THIRD EDITION

THE NATURAL SPEAKER

Randy Fujishin
West Valley College

Allyn & Bacon
Boston • London • Toronto • Sydney • Tokyo • Singapore

Series Editor: Karon Bowers
Editorial Assistant: Scout Reilly
Marketing Manager: Jackie Aaron
Production Coordinator: Susan Brown
Editorial-Production Service: Matrix Productions
Cover Administrator: Jennifer Hart
Composition Buyer: Linda Cox
Manufacturing Buyer: Megan Cochran

Copyright © 2000, 1997, 1994 by Allyn & Bacon
A Pearson Education Company
Needham Heights, Mass. 02494

www.abacon.com

Library of Congress Cataloging-in-Publication Data

Fujishin, Randy.
    The natural speaker / Randy Fujishin. – 3rd ed.
      p. cm.
    Includes index.
    ISBN 0-205-29575-4
    1. Public speaking. I. Title
PN4121.F77 1999
808.5'1–dc21   98-54258
                          CIP

Printed in the United States of America

10 9 8 7 6 5 4 3   03 02 01 00

For Dad

CONTENTS

PREFACE

We all have our own natural way of breathing, walking, seeing, and talking. Some of us, when we talk, like to tell stories, while others prefer facts and figures. Some boast dynamic, commanding voices, and others offer gentle, soothing tones. There are those who speak quickly and those who prefer to stroll through their sentences. Over the years, these individual tendencies become part of our natural style—a large part of who we are.

Yet, when asked to speak before an audience, most of us are anything but ourselves. We change in immediate and dramatic ways. Our bodies become tense, our thinking is disjointed, and our hearts are overwhelmed with fear. We can hardly think about giving a speech without falling over.

This book is a guide that will help you give a speech without falling over. It will enhance and improve your natural speaking strengths, while providing you with a basic knowledge of speech construction, practice, and delivery. We'll let the natural speaker inside you come out in the process of developing these skills.

Chapters 1 and 2 explore the nature and principles of communication, your communication attitude, and five interpersonal communication skills that are vital to effective communication in your everyday life. You are also encouraged to give yourself permission to grow in all these areas. Chapter 3 introduces you to the basic components and skills necessary for giving your first speech.

Chapters 4, 5, and 6 address selecting a speech topic, gathering your material, and organizing any speech topic. In these chapters, you are given a practical guide to constructing a speech from start to finish in an effective and comprehensive way.

Chapter 7, highlights the physical components of speaker delivery and gives practical methods for delivery improvement. The emphasis of this chapter is on developing those speaking strengths you already possess, and adding new skills that will enhance your natural style.

Chapter 8 covers the principles of sharing information with your audience. Also presented are practical suggestions for informative speaking, language use, and answering audience questions. Chapter 9 examines the fundamentals of persuasive speaking. Aristotle's three persuasive appeals—ethos, logos, and pathos—are discussed, and ways you can incorporate each appeal into your speech are presented.

Finally, Chapter 10 explores the idea that your role as a public speaker could last your entire lifetime and is not limited to one class experience. By continuing to use your public speaking skills in your professional, educational, and personal life, you will discover a deepening awareness and appreciation of who you are and what you can share with others. This chapter concludes with a five-step process for giving impromptu speeches—the most common type of speech you will deliver in your lifetime.

The purpose of this book is to give you the basic skills to present a speech to any audience in a way that is natural, effective, and rewarding for you. Your decision to develop and improve your natural speaking abilities is one that will reward you, both professionally and personally, for the rest of your life.

I wish to acknowledge the helpful comments of the reviewers of this edition: Blanton Croft, Northern Virginia Community College; Martha Einerson, University of Idaho; Kathleen Romanos, North Shore Community College; and Archie Wortham, St. Philip's College.

I also wish to acknowledge my four sisters, Diane, Melanie, Nanette, and Teresa for their support and love for as long as I can remember. My mother, for her constant love and blessings. My wife, Vicky, for being my most precious gift in this lifetime. Our sons, Tyler and Jared, for teaching us what joy is all about. My good friend, Paul, for being my brother. And finally, my father, who taught me to love family, to work hard, and to get up early in the morning. It is to his loving memory that I dedicate this book.

Randy Fujishin

1

COMMUNICATING WITH OTHERS
Your Most Important Skill

Never before had Paul sat so long in total silence with another human being. Paul, a young psychologist, was in a therapy session with his client, a middle-aged woman with lifeless eyes, arms that hung limply at her side, and a posture that displayed the shame and anger that often accompanies victims of physical abuse.

It was during Paul's first year of clinical training as a marriage, family, and child therapist that he had worked with her. The woman came to therapy with a long history of depression and withdrawal. As a novice therapist, Paul encouraged her to open up and share her feelings. But all the woman did was sit in silence during those first two sessions. He asked the usual questions therapists are trained to ask, and she responded only with silence. She simply stared out the window to the peaceful mountains in the distance, as they sat in his cramped little office.

During the course of therapy, she did make some progress. After two months, she responded in short sentences to some of Paul's questions. She even smiled a time or two. Yet, within four months, she quit coming to her sessions. Paul left messages on her answering machine inviting her back to therapy, but she did not respond. Paul never saw the woman again.

To this day, Paul is haunted by something she said at the end of one of her final sessions. After he asked her why she spent the vast majority of her time in therapy in silence, she slowly admitted, "Most times it's less painful to be silent than to talk. I think it would be much easier to live my entire life not having to communicate with anyone."

Can you imagine a life without communication? Immediately your existence would change in dramatic ways, leaving you with an entirely different life. An empty, hollow life.

No longer could you talk with friends over coffee or laugh with your family at a picnic. No longer could you whisper sweet nothings to your spouse or discuss the latest movie with a neighbor. No longer could you debate an issue at a business meeting or negotiate the price of a used car. No longer could you apologize for a wrong or ask for forgiveness from a wounded friend. In short, no longer would you be fully human. We need communication as a bridge to others in this life.

Hell was once described, not as a burning pit of endless agony, but as a cold, lonely, isolated place where each person was sentenced to spend eternity alone on an island. No bridges between the islands. No way to span the gulf between people. Forever alone. A life without communication would be hell.

WHAT IS COMMUNICATION?

Although there are numerous definitions for communication, the following definition is very simple and has been around for a long time. *Communication* is the process of sending and receiving messages. The sender sends a message through a channel to a receiver. The receiver responds with feedback to the sender, and noise can interfere with the fidelity or accuracy of the message. Communication can be both verbal and nonverbal. *Verbal* communication consists of all language that is spoken and written, whereas *nonverbal* communication is all communication that is not spoken or written.

THE SIX COMPONENTS OF COMMUNICATION

The communication process is made up of six components. They are the sender, message, channel, receiver, feedback, and noise.

Sender

The *sender* is the originator of the message. In other models of communication, the sender can also be called the source of the message. The process of communication begins at this point with a speaker who wishes to communicate an idea or feeling. It's important to note the sender doesn't simply send a message. She must first decide what she wants to communicate and then encode the message. *Encoding* is the process of converting the message into language and terms that will be understood by the receiver. Once the message is encoded, it is sent to the receiver.

Message

The idea or feeling the sender wants to communicate is called the *message*. The message can be any idea, thought, emotion, or feeling the sender wishes to communicate. Whether it's a flirtatious wink across a crowded room or a college commencement address, the message is still the thought or feeling the sender wants to communicate.

Channel

The *channel* is the means by which a message is transmitted. Messages can be transmitted through channels of hearing, sight, smell, taste, and touch. A sender can use a variety of channels to communicate her message. For instance, if she wants to communicate affection to someone special, she can choose to tell the person with words, hug the person, send cookies, write a letter, or offer perfume. In public speaking, the auditory and visual channels are used most often. But it's important to keep in mind that the more channels utilized by the sender, the more impact the message has on the receiver.

Receiver

The destination of the message is called the *receiver*. Without the receiver, communication does not occur. In public speaking, the receiver of the message is the audience. In the communication model, the receiver receives the message, then must decode the message. *Decoding* is the process of translating the message so that it has meaning for the receiver. A wink of the eye from the sender can be decoded or interpreted in many ways. It can be a nonverbal sign of flirting, a sign there's dust in the eye, or even the first symptom of an epileptic seizure. The decoding process is vital in communication.

Feedback

The response of the receiver to the sender is called *feedback*. Although feedback is really a message from the receiver to the sender, the term helps us see the circular movement of this communication model. It should be stressed that the receiver can send the return message through all the same channel options as the sender when she encodes and sends the response.

Noise

Noise is any disturbance or interference in the communication process. *External noise* is any physical interference that diminishes or reduces the meaning of the message. Examples of external noise include background talking, a jackhammer banging outside the building, or even a distracting mannerism of the speaker. All these and more can interfere with the communication process. Psychological or semantic interference, on the other hand, is called *internal noise*. Internal noise can cause us to misinterpret or decode the message in a way not intended. A word with multiple meanings is a common example of internal noise. For instance, an audience may interpret the speaker's statement, "In Japan, students respect their teachers," in a variety of ways depending on their individual interpretations of the word "respect."

THE PRINCIPLES OF COMMUNICATION

Now that you have an idea of what communication is and the elements that make up the process, you are in a better position to examine some principles that govern communication.

You Cannot Not Communicate

Even when you don't think you're communicating, your nonverbal behavior is constantly giving off important messages. Your posture, your eye contact or lack of it, and the manner in which you walk or even sleep send messages loaded with meaning to the outside observer. Freud wisely observed, "He who has eyes to see and ears to hear may convince himself that no mortal can keep a secret. If his lips are silent, he chatters with his finger tips and betrayal oozes out of him at every pore."[1] Your body, your movements, your use of time, the distance you stand from others, and even your clothes closet broadcast constant and powerful messages to observers. You are always communicating.

Communication Is Irreversible

Many times we wish we could retract a critical word or erase an angry response that we have made. Unfortunately, this is not possible. An apology for harsh words can be sincerely accepted, but the memory of the event can live on for the remainder of a person's life. Human memory is a funny thing. The least of gestures, the smallest of words can haunt us long after the event. It might be wise for us to remember the recommendation, "One seldom regrets unspoken words."

Communication Is a Process

Many years ago, Heraclitus observed, "You never step into the same river twice." The river has changed—the water clarity is different, the temperature is different, the current is different, the depth is different, and the width is different. The river may look the same, but it's a different river. In fact, you too have changed—the very cells of your body are different—since you last stepped into its waters.

This same principle holds true for communication. A smile might have worked while requesting something from a friend last week. But this week, the same smile elicits mild rejection. Why? Because you cannot repeat any event in exactly the same manner. Things have changed. Both participants have changed in countless subtle and not so subtle ways. It is impossible to replicate the hundreds of minute variables influencing you just a week ago. Everything has changed to some degree during the week.

Have you ever seen the same movie twice? It's amazing how many new things you see the second time around that went unnoticed during your first viewing. Your emotional response to the film may also have changed, because of the personal changes and emotional experiences you have had since you first saw the movie.

Communication is a process. Life is a process. The soldier who goes off to war returns a different person. The old woman dying in the city hospital bed is not the same person who ran along the country lane 70 years ago. That is, however, the beauty of life. We can explore, experiment, change, and grow as we get older, so that on our deathbed we will have very few regrets.

Communication Is Learned

There are some nonverbal communication behaviors that seem to be universal, such as smiling and crying. But the majority of verbal and nonverbal communication is learned. The specific language that a child grows up with is learned early in childhood, as are the nonverbal communication behaviors that are appropriate for a specific culture. For instance, in the American culture we value and encourage direct eye contact, especially in the public speaking arena. Yet, a native of the Japanese culture would interpret the same direct eye contact as a sign of rudeness and lack of respect, especially when the speaker is addressing an individual of higher status.

Just as a fish is unaware of the water surrounding it, an individual might not be aware that communication is learned, because he too is surrounded by the language and culture of his society. However, when a person learns a new language, visits a foreign country, or acquaints himself with a person from a different culture, he begins to realize that his way of talking and perceiving the world is but one of many. There are many realities out there, and perhaps one important indicator of maturity is the realization that "our way" isn't necessarily the only or best way.

The most important aspect of this principle is that ineffective ways of communicating can be replaced by learning new, more effective methods of communicating. Often people think that because they can talk, they can communicate effectively too. This is far from the truth. Ernest Hemingway once warned us "not to confuse motion for action." The same holds true for talking and communicating. Communicating effectively in our interpersonal and professional lives requires study and practice. Effective communication skills can be learned. They must be learned if we are to experience a life that is meaningful and worth living.

Communication Needs to Be Cross-Culturally Appreciated

Perhaps the most significant lesson we can learn is that communication is often culture specific. Granted, the principles of communication mentioned thus far apply to all cultures. Individuals from all cultures learn to communicate. They cannot not communicate. Their communication and their lives are in process. And once they communicate a message, intentionally or unintentionally, the effect is irreversibly felt by others.

But we must not make the mistake of thinking that what we value in terms of communication competencies is desired by all people in every culture. This is not always the case. For example, in this book you will be encouraged to maintain direct eye contact with your listeners, use expressive gestures, employ vocal variety, and share personal illustrations in your speaking. For the purposes of addressing most American audiences, these and other skills will serve a positive and desirable function. But if you were addressing a group of Japanese businessmen in Tokyo, these same behaviors might be interpreted as overly forward, disrespectful, annoying, and even rude. The Japanese often view direct eye contact as an invasion of personal space. The use of exaggerated gestures and vocal variety does not fit their more restrained and formal style of communication. And personal disclosure would be inappropriate, if not suspect, in a large group of strangers.

"Well," you sigh, "I just won't ever give a speech to a group of Japanese businessmen in Tokyo!" Maybe not, but the United States is a country that is home to hundreds of different cultures. That's the beauty of our nation! If you really analyzed any audience in America, you'd be surprised at the heterogeneous mix of the various cultures and ethnic backgrounds of your listeners.

The purpose of this public speaking book is not to provide you with a list of the communication skills and behaviors valued by each of these different cultures. We'll leave that book to someone else. But you are encouraged to become aware of, sensitive to, and respectful of these differences. This is not to say you must shift your communication style with each audience you address. That would be an impossible task. But you are being challenged to examine the notion that "your way is the only way."

You need to become more aware of the subtle, and not so subtle, differences between cultures. Not only must you raise your level of awareness concerning these differences, but you also need to be more sensitive to them, not only in your speaking, but in your daily interactions with others. And finally, you must respect these differences in your speaking and listening with all people. The next section will help you meet this challenge.

ATTITUDE IS MORE IMPORTANT THAN APTITUDE

Before proceeding to the next chapter, the attitude of the communicator needs to be mentioned, for it is the attitude of the speaker that ranks as the most important factor in effective communication.

A person's attitude is far more important than his aptitude in communicating with others. An individual can be highly trained and skilled in the communication arts, but may possess an angry or critical attitude. It's this negative attitude that is sensed below the level of spoken language, and the receiver or audience ultimately responds to it, rather than to the words.

The attitudes that distinguish truly effective communicators from less effective ones are worth mentioning here. Effective communicators seem to possess an attitude of self-acceptance. They accept who they are without having to prove a great deal to others. They exhibit an attitude of other-centeredness, which enables them to empathize with, care for, and respond to others. Rather than constantly being consumed with the need or desire to control others or gain their approval, these self-accepting individuals can dance to the beat of a different drummer with greater ease and grace. They don't spend a lot of time looking over their shoulders or down their noses.

Flexibility is another attitude that characterizes these individuals, for they are more likely to experiment with new behaviors, to take risks, and to make mistakes. They appear to be gentle in their dealings with others. And finally, these individuals possess a sense of openness and authenticity that makes them comfortable to be around, demanding little energy. We walk away from these individuals feeling enlarged rather than diminished.

The most telling attitude of effective communicators is their sense of joy—not just a temporary happiness or a practiced, interpersonal warmth, but a joyfulness that seems to come from deep within. Usually these individuals have lived a while, they have managed to survive and accept some of life's tragedies, and still, they have chosen to embrace the beauty and mystery of life.

You know when you've been in their presence, for they usually make you feel calm, relaxed, and trusting. Just as certain animals can sense fear in some people and love in others, you can feel the attitude of joyfulness in these individuals. At such times, words really don't matter all that much.

Without these positive attitudes shaping and influencing the communication process, most communication skills training is wasted. Ultimately, the heart is more important than the head.

COMMUNICATION SKILLS FOR YOUR LIFE

Before we actually begin learning about the concepts and skills of effective public speaking, let's spend a few moments examining your personal communication life.

There have been individuals who were powerful, persuasive public speakers. They could command the attention of hundreds of people with their words alone. Their relationship with the audience was impressive, as the masses swayed in unison to their every word.

But their relationship with the audience wasn't necessarily indicative of their relationships with individuals in their personal lives. Some of these outstanding public speakers had miserable personal lives, wracked with pain, emptiness, and longing. Their awesome speaking skills could impress hundreds in the audience but could do very little to bridge the gulf between themselves and those who should have mattered—family and friends.

In this book you will learn skills and concepts that will help you speak effectively to an audience. But before you run out and book speaking engagements, we need to begin with a brief discussion on a topic that is enormously important to your life—your interpersonal communication impact on others.

Every time you talk with someone, you either enlarge or diminish that person by your interaction. Suppose that you and another person are engaged in casual conversation for a few minutes and then you say good-bye. As you walk away from that individual, how are you feeling? What kind of emotional impact did he have on you? Maybe he had a diminishing impact, and you say to yourself, "Yuk! I'm glad to be away from that negative, depressing guy. I was feeling all right before I talked with him." Perhaps he didn't have any noticeable impact on you, and you're saying, "I wonder where I parked that darn car of mine." Or just maybe, his impact on you was enlarging, and you're exclaiming, "I felt pretty down before I talked with him, and now I feel better. The world doesn't look as depressing as it did just a few minutes ago."

Do others enlarge or diminish you? Don't count the neutral impact as a third category, because no impact is similar to a negative impact. So clump those two together into the "diminish" category. If you still want three categories, that's okay. The discussion will work either way.

Remember that communication is a process, and your past history, your state of mind, your physical condition, and a host of other factors come into play here. And yet, ultimately, you have an impact on others every time you interact. You either enlarge or diminish another person by your interactions. With every word, sound, gesture, expression, glance, movement, pause, and touch you share with another person, he or she is changed in ways that are both subtle and striking.

There are five specific ways you can enlarge others by your interpersonal communication with them: not taking communication so personally, listening without verbal interruption, listening reflectively, reframing, and touching.

Not Taking Communication So Personally

Most of us listen to what others say in terms of how it affects us personally. We ask questions such as: "Is that right or wrong (from *my* point of view)?" "How does that affect *me*?" "What does the speaker think/feel about *me*?" "How do *I* feel about what was shared?" "How do *I* respond?" In all these questions, did you notice where the focus of attention was? It was on our response, our evaluation, our point of view—in short, we take center stage; everything revolves around us. We take it all so personally.

Now, that's not necessarily bad. We need to evaluate the merits of a sales presentation, we need to form an opinion of our new manager, and we need to check our emotional response in a conflict situation. But to overemphasize a self-centered approach to all communication is not healthy. We need to develop the ability to suspend judgment when listening to another person. We need to develop the art of psychological and emotional disengagement—to take our ego out of gear once in a while. When we always take what is said personally, we get hooked into many unnecessary arguments, conflicts, and struggles.

An effective technique that helps disengage your ego, and not take everything that is said so personally, is to ask these questions when you're listening to someone else:

"What is this person's point of view?"
"What does this say about this person?"
"How is this person feeling?"
"Where is this person coming from?"
"How does this person see the situation?"
"Who is this person?"

Did you notice the different focus of attention? No longer do we take center stage. The speaker is the focus of attention—her point of view, her feelings, her frame of reference, her character and personality. We're not taking in all that is said in terms of how it affects us. We are broadening our perspective to include the one who is talking. We have concentrated on the speaker, and consequently, we have also distanced ourselves from her. We are not taking her communication so personally.

The ability to not take communication personally is the first step in communication—to be able to hear what the other person is saying without a screen of self-centered questions filtering and clouding what is being said. Without this ability, communication with others will be superficial and often defensive. Without this ability, we will be hearing only the echoes of our own mind, instead of the thoughts and feelings of the other person.

Listening without Verbal Interruption

Now that we can accept what is being said from an other-centered point of view, we can begin to listen without verbal interruption—the ability to be silent for a period of time when someone else is speaking.

Did you know that when we are talking with another person, we verbally interrupt the other person every 12 seconds? Every 12 seconds! "That's wonderful!" "That's terrible!" "I'm sure!" "I'm all..." "That reminds me of a time when I..." "If I were you, I would..." "No, that's not true, because..." "Well, it was even worse for me, because I..." and the interruptions go on and on.... Every 12 seconds. Back and forth.... On and on we interrupt.

And we wonder why we don't feel like we've been really listened to, really taken seriously, really understood at a deep level by the end of the day. Because of the constant interruptions and judgments, advice and direction, we realize there is no safe harbor to simply say what's on our minds and in our hearts without being interrupted from all sides every

12 seconds. Maybe that explains why we pay certain people $75 to $125 an hour to just sit quietly and listen to us in therapy.

One of the most enlarging behaviors we can share with another person is to listen without verbal evaluation—without interrupting every 12 seconds! What an oasis that would be. Perhaps the most loving thing we can do for another human being is to listen quietly, deeply, without interruption.

The next time your spouse, your child, or a neighbor begins talking with you, ask yourself the question, "Should I give this person 12 seconds before I interrupt, or should I allow 120 seconds?" If you wear a watch with a sweep second hand, time yourself if you can do it without being too obvious. See what happens if you remain silent for two entire minutes! Many times the other person won't even notice your silence and will continue talking. Other times, he might ask, "Is something wrong?" "Are you all right?" Such questions could be indicators that the other person is accustomed to your interruptions. Don't feel bad. Just respond by saying, "Everything is fine. I just think what you're saying is important, and I didn't want to interrupt you."

Listening Reflectively

In addition to not taking communication too personally and listening without verbal interruption, another enlarging communication behavior is to listen reflectively. To listen *reflectively* means to mirror back to the speaker what he is saying.

When you are listening to someone, think in terms of, "What is this person trying to communicate to me?" "What is this person saying?" "What is this person feeling?" As you begin to get a sense of exactly what this person is attempting to communicate to you, check it out—reflect or mirror back to the speaker. The simplest way to accomplish this is to begin your questions with:

"Are you saying...?"
"I hear you saying...?"
"You think...?"
"You believe...?"
"Are you feeling...?"
"Your point is...?
"Do you mean...?"

These are simple beginnings to your questions, but they will change the entire focus of your communication. Once again, where is the attention directed? You? Or the other person? Right, the other person! Now you're getting it.

With practice, this reflective way of listening will become quite natural, and you will notice that your communication patterns will shift from a self-centered posture to a more other-centered focus. Very often there will be a change in the relationship with this person if reflective listening is used with any frequency.

There are numerous advantages of this reflective listening technique. First, it shifts the focus from you to the speaker, and it encourages you to not take communication too personally. Hopefully, it will also force you to listen without verbal judgment. Second, reflective listening will prove to the speaker that you care about what he is saying. This, in and of itself, is enlarging. Third, it improves the accuracy of communication. If your reflected statement is inaccurate, the speaker can clarify, explain, or illustrate in detail. Fourth, this type of listening takes the burden off you. No longer do you have to judge, give advice, or solve problems. You are simply acting as a mirror, reflecting the other person's image back to him. Fifth, you provide the speaker with a safe harbor where he can talk and be heard. It beats paying $75 to $125 an hour just to be heard accurately.

Reframing What Is Said

A fourth way you can enlarge a person is to reframe his negative perception of a situation, circumstance, or person. The *reframing* technique involves seeing something from a different perspective or point of view. Montaigne once cautioned, "We are hurt not so much by what happens, as by our opinion of what happens." In other words, our perceptions of an event are more important than the event itself.

How we choose to see something is instrumental in determining how we will respond to, deal with, and resolve problems that confront us. For instance, a man is fired from his job. Nothing can change the fact that he has been fired. But he can view the event from a variety of perspectives. The obvious viewpoint is that the firing is a terrible thing. He is out of employment. He will need to begin looking for another job. It's a depressing situation. Many would stop here, go no further in their attempt to see this event from a different point of view, and simply become hurt, angry, or depressed. Many people do not realize there can be other ways of perceiving this same event.

It can be seen as a new beginning. He can finally pursue employment that might be more to his liking. It can be seen as a learning experience. What went wrong? How can he improve? What skills does he need to develop for future jobs? It can be viewed as a chance to take a break from the rat race. If he can afford it, he can use the next few weeks or months to rest, and possibly take a vacation from the responsibilities of earning a living. It can be seen as a time to travel. He can sell everything he owns and hit the road. It can be viewed as an opportunity to be creative and start his own little company or business. This one event can be seen in a hundred different ways—no one way more valid than another.

Despite the numerous points of view from which we can choose to see a situation, we tend to get stuck with the first interpretation that pops into our heads. We cement that perspective into our field of vision and limit our emotional responses to that point of view. In short, we get stuck. One experienced marriage and family therapist stated, "As a counselor, I don't change my clients' situation; I simply help them see other ways of viewing the same situation." This seems to have a freeing effect on clients. It releases them from the bondage of seeing something from only one point of view. Depression can also be viewed as an invitation to grow. Anger can also be seen as a way of dealing with repressed sadness. Death of a loved one can also be a reminder to love those around us with greater appreciation. There are many ways of seeing. We need to be flexible in our perceptions and interpretations of those events that make up the fabric of our lives.

As a friend, you can enlarge others by opening their eyes to other ways of viewing a situation. If they share something "terrible" that has just happened to them, you can listen without verbal interruption, reflect what they are saying and feeling, and if you can, reframe their situation. You can do this by simply stating:

"John, another way of looking at this is…"
"Mary, could this also mean…"
"Tuan, another interpretation of this is…"

Your reframing doesn't have to be accepted by others as the truth, as insightful, or even as a solution to a problem. It's simply a way of allowing them not to get stuck with their own frame of reference. The purpose is to get them unstuck. To help them see with a different set of glasses. To assist them in looking at the same situation from a different perspective. You can be instrumental in freeing them from the prison of their own perceptions.

Touching Others

The final way to enlarge others is to touch them. This sounds like an obvious suggestion, but it's often overlooked as a means of making others feel acknowledged, cared for, and loved. There are times when words ring hollow and we need the comfort and reassurance that only physical contact can provide.

A little boy was frightened by a summer thunderstorm and ran to his father for comfort. The father attempted to reassure the boy by saying that the lightning and thunder were actually far away. "Anyway," added the dad, "God will always be with you for protection even though you can't see him." The boy listened to his father, but continued to crawl up onto his lap. "I know that," the boy said, "but can I hug you anyway? I need something with skin on it."

At the end of the nineteenth century in Europe, orphaned children under the age of six months were dying for some unknown reason. The mortality rate for these infants in the orphanages of Europe was 100 percent.[2] The experts tried to help by giving the infants more food, better lighting, special medicines, and even soothing music. But nothing seemed to work. The babies kept dying. This was so prevalent in Europe that it was referred to as the "Marasmus Syndrome." *Marasmus* in Latin means "to waste away." And that's what the babies continued to do—waste away. Apparently, these infants didn't possess the will to begin life. Then the orphanages discovered that if these young infants were touched on a regular basis by "hired mothers"—women who were paid to handle, cuddle, and fondle the babies—they would live. The death rate dropped to the point at which an infant's death was the exception.

Could it be that we suffer from an adult form of the Marasmus Syndrome? Perhaps in our culture, we are wasting away from lack of touch. How many hugs do you receive a day? When was the last time you really hugged another human being for more than one or two seconds? One of the most powerful ways to enlarge another person is to touch them. Touching changes relationships. It changes lives.

There are entire books devoted to the importance of touching behavior, but for our purposes, remember there are times when words don't bridge the gap between you and another person. When to touch? How long to touch? How to touch? These are questions only you can answer depending on the individual, the situation, and your intent. But keep in mind that touching others is one of the most powerful ways that we enlarge others, and ourselves.

COMMUNICATION ACTIVITIES

Personal Activities

1. **Enlarging communication behaviors**

   On a sheet of paper, identify three individuals whose communication behaviors have had an enlarging impact on your life. List specific behaviors that each person has demonstrated. If possible, thank each of the three individuals for their positive contributions to your life.

2. Communicating in other cultures

Ask an individual from a different cultural background about his or her communication behaviors and attitudes. How does his or her behaviors and attitudes differ from your own? How are they similar? How did you feel about communicating with a person from a different cultural background?

Class Activities

1. Analyzing a communication event

Consider a recent communication event from your life—asking a friend for a favor, trying to persuade your employer for a raise, or resolving a relationship conflict. Identify the six communication components of sender, message, channel, receiver, feedback, and noise, and explain how they contributed to the success or failure of the communication event. Be prepared to discuss your thoughts and feelings about this assignment in class.

2. Listening to others

Use reflective listening when you are talking with a friend. After they have completed a statement, try reflecting it back to them ("Are you saying...?" or "Do you mean to tell me that...?"). How did it feel? How did your friend respond to your mirroring? Be prepared to discuss your reactions to this assignment in class.

NOTES

1. Sigmund Freud, *A General Introduction to Psychoanalysis* (New York: Garden City Publishing Co., 1938).
2. Ashley Montague, *Touching: The Significance of the Skin* (New York: Columbia University Press, 1971).

2

GIVING YOURSELF PERMISSION
Welcoming a New You

Randy was the coward. The others were just as inexperienced, anxious, and fearful as he, but Randy stayed home pretending to be sick, while the other four students went to their fate on that terrible spring day many years ago.

It was the day the five finalists for student body president of Campbell Junior High were to deliver their campaign speeches to the all-school assembly. The five young candidates were told the speeches were not to exceed seven minutes, and the only other requirement placed on them was to sit quietly and not make silly faces to the audience as they waited onstage for their turn to speak.

Simple enough, Randy thought. But the three weeks that preceded that speech day were perhaps the worst of his life. As a seventh grader, he hadn't the slightest idea what he should say or how he should say it.

To make matters worse, Randy stuttered a little. He stuttered only when he got nervous, but it was a definite stutter. He would try to race through his sentences, only to trip on the third or fourth word. Then the pattern was always the same. His face would get hot, his vision would blur, and he would become extremely embarrassed and wish he were dead. But somehow, he had managed to get through school without any major confrontations. At least, until this speech.

After many hours of painful writing, Randy's speech was neatly written in blue ink on lined yellow paper. It wasn't a memorable or stirring speech. It mentioned something about making the school the greatest junior high in the world and, at the same time, promised to reduce the price of popcorn and cokes at school dances. He knew the other candidates probably had better speeches, but he had tried his best.

Well, the day before the all-school assembly, Randy gave his neatly written speech to Chuck, an eighth grader he played football with, and told him he felt like he was coming down with the flu. Randy asked Chuck if he would read his speech at the assembly, just in case he was too sick to come to school that next day. Chuck volunteered enthusiastically, as he was a performer at heart. And Randy, relieved and a little ashamed, quickly said good-bye to his friend.

The next day came, and Randy didn't go to school. He missed the all-school assembly and missed giving his first speech. Randy felt guilty for telling his mom he was sick when he really wasn't. He felt ashamed for not giving the speech. And he even felt bad that Chuck had to speak in his place. All this emotional turmoil simply over one speech. But at least he didn't have to speak.

However, things got worse. Randy was even more depressed the following Tuesday, election day, when he learned he had been elected student body president of Campbell Junior High School! There was no escape. The prospect of delivering four speeches to the student body during the next school year was simply overwhelming. He couldn't face the possibility of reliving this terrible experience again. He wanted to die.

THE ONLY WAY WE GROW

That summer was a turning point for Randy. He didn't resign from his newly won office. He even smiled when students congratulated him during those final days before summer vacation began. Yet he burned inside with fear. How was he going to get out of giving those four speeches next fall?

Not one day that summer went by without waves of dread rolling over Randy as he wrestled with the thought of having to give speeches during the upcoming school year. He could be sick on those speaking days. Maybe he could have Chuck talk for him again. But something told Randy that this was a very important issue in his life, and he needed to face it. He was trapped.

Mr. Hillard was a kind and wise man in the neighborhood. He was about 65, with large hands, and a gentle wife who gave Randy orange juice to drink every time he mowed their lawn on Saturdays. Randy was paid a couple of dollars to mow their front and back lawns. What Randy remembered most was that he always left the Hillards' house feeling better than he had before he arrived. Mr. and Mrs. Hillard were loving people.

Randy didn't know what made him tell Mr. Hillard about his predicament that summer. Maybe he felt safe around this older man. But when he described his situation to him, Mr. Hillard only smiled. Randy talked on and on about how he might not speak well at the assemblies. How he might stutter and the students would think he was stupid. How he would probably make a fool of himself. They would all discover what a fraud he really was. After Randy finished sharing his worries, Mr. Hillard smiled again, but said nothing.

There was a long silence as Mr. Hillard stared at the grass. "That was a pretty good speech you just gave," the old man began. "I liked that you were speaking from your heart. That's the only kind of speaking that moves me," Mr. Hillard continued. "But I do have a suggestion," he ventured. "You should give yourself permission to make some mistakes in your life. Give yourself permission to not be perfect. That's the only way we grow."

That summer was a good one for Randy. He mowed the Hillards' lawn on those warm Saturday mornings, drank Mrs. Hillard's freshly squeezed orange juice, and talked Mr. Hillard's ears off as they sat in the cool breezeway when the work was done. That was the summer that Randy and Mr. Hillard dug up the old junipers that lined the front driveway and planted new shrubs in their place. That was the summer that Mr. Hillard listened to the young boy with his entire heart. And that was the summer Randy would never forget, long after Mr. Hillard was gone.

Randy gave four speeches that following autumn. They weren't great. But he did show up. And no one else spoke for him. Randy even discovered that his stuttering diminished somewhat, once he gave himself permission to make mistakes.

GIVING YOURSELF PERMISSION TO MAKE MISTAKES

Someone once said, "If you're not failing every once in a while, you're living life too cautiously." One of the primary stumbling blocks to our personal growth is our fear of making a mistake. Making the wrong decision. Choosing the wrong profession. Marrying the wrong person. Looking foolish in the eyes of others. We are often paralyzed into not acting at all, not taking any step, because we fear it might be the wrong one.

But aren't mistakes an important part of the learning process? Isn't that how we truly learn something? Not from reading it in a book or listening to someone else, but by experiencing it ourselves. The first time we tried to walk as infants was probably awkward, if not humorous. And our initial attempt at riding a bicycle without mom or dad holding on to the seat must have been a sight. Remember, we learn from our mistakes. That's the beauty of this journey.

The now-famous R. H. Macy, founder of Macy's Department Stores, tried seven times to get his department stores started, but failed each time. Can you imagine his sense of failure even after the first or second attempt? But on the eighth venture out, he succeeded. Just think of all the Macy's stores you've visited over the years. Would you have had the courage to risk even a second attempt, let alone an eighth? The saddest thing is not that we didn't succeed, but rather that we didn't even try. We learn from our mistakes.

As you read this book, you will be asked to try new behaviors and new ways of seeing yourself. Don't take yourself too seriously on this journey. Give yourself permission to make mistakes along the way. Give yourself permission to be gentle on yourself.

A PERMISSION LIST FOR SPEAKERS

Before we begin talking about the mechanics of speaking in front of others, we need to take a few moments to examine your attitudes toward public speaking. People will often train as public speakers without ever once asking themselves if this is a skill they would like to improve. They struggle through all the preparation and practice required for effective public speaking, and yet, they neglect to explore some very fundamental issues involved in this highly charged communication event. They never give themselves permission to improve their speaking skills.

This may sound strange to you—giving yourself permission to improve your speaking skills. Usually, public speaking training is imposed on you by someone else. It's required by your college or university for graduation, or your manager at work feels you would benefit from such a course. Rarely do you, after an afternoon of introspection, decide suddenly that your speaking skills are lacking and your life would be dramatically improved if you learned to speak more effectively on your feet.

So, let's take a few moments to explore this whole area of giving yourself permission to speak. Read the following statements, and circle the response that most accurately describes your feelings.

1. I give myself permission to express myself.   yes/no/unsure
2. I give myself permission to stand up in front   yes/no/unsure
   of others.
3. I give myself permission to ask others to listen   yes/no/unsure
   to me.
4. I give myself permission to experience something   yes/no/unsure
   new.
5. I give myself permission to feel uncomfortable.   yes/no/unsure
6. I give myself permission to speak in front of others. yes/no/unsure
7. I give myself permission to not be perfect.   yes/no/unsure

8. I give myself permission to make mistakes.   yes/no/unsure
9. I give myself permission to try new speaking   yes/no/unsure
   skills.
10. I give myself permission to improve my speaking.   yes/no/unsure
11. I give myself permission to not know all   yes/no/unsure
    the answers.
12. I give myself permission to teach others.   yes/no/unsure
13. I give myself permission to persuade others.   yes/no/unsure
14. I give myself permission to let others have their   yes/no/unsure
    opinions.
15. I give myself permission not to seek the approval   yes/no/unsure
    of others.
16. I give myself permission to enjoy my time speaking   yes/no/unsure
    in public.
17. I give myself permission to like my voice and   yes/no/unsure
    my body.
18. I give myself permission to be gentle on myself.   yes/no/unsure
19. I give myself permission to be myself.   yes/no/unsure
20. I give myself permission to love myself.   yes/no/unsure

Did it feel unusual or unnatural "giving yourself permission" to do or feel these things? Usually permission to think, feel, or do something comes from someone or something outside yourself. It comes from the government, the boss, the teacher, the church, the school, your parents, your friends, or your spouse.

However, in the 20 permission statements you just considered, the permission was coming from *you,* not someone else. It didn't matter whether you responded with "yes," "no," or "unsure," because it was you who was doing the deciding. No one else. You were the one who was giving permission or not giving permission. You were even the person deciding if you were "unsure" about each statement. No matter how you responded, each of the 20 times, you were in the control tower deciding how each decision landed.

This concept of where permission resides is often called the *locus of power.* Do you decide things for yourself, or do others decide for you? It's the subtle difference between "I have to…" and "I choose to…." Try this. In a normal speaking voice say, "I *have* to give a speech." Say it again. How did that feel? Now try saying, "I *choose* to give a speech." Again. How did that feel? Did you notice a difference between the two statements?

With the "I have to" statement, you may have noticed less commitment in your voice, perhaps even less energy. When you said, "I choose to give a speech," you may have felt more definite, more determined. If not, try the "choose" statement again. Feel anything different? If you think that feels awkward or strange, try saying "I choose not to give a speech" a couple of times and explore how that statement feels to you.

You might be thinking they're just words—"I have to...," "I choose to...," and "I choose not to...." But words are powerful, and these particular words, "have to" and "choose to," bring you to an interesting place in your personal decision making. Who makes your decisions? Are they made for you most of the time (I have to...)? Or do you choose and decide for yourself (I choose to...; I choose not to...)?

Much of your sense of independence, personal strength, and internal resilience depends directly upon your decision to think and decide for yourself during your lifetime.

As you marked your responses to the 20 permission list items, you may have been surprised by the number of statements you have never consciously considered before this moment. These are not questions we often ask ourselves. And it would not be unusual if you responded more frequently with "no" and "unsure" than "yes," because most individuals often feel they have nothing really important to share that would warrant the attention of a group of human beings. Many people, after taking this questionnaire, report they rarely feel anyone would want to listen to them speak.

If your answer to these items was "yes" the majority of the time, you are the exception to the rule, and your training in public speaking should be easy, if not downright enjoyable. If, however, you were unsure, responding with lots of nos, or you thought this was a dumb set of questions, don't be discouraged. Your training in public speaking might just change your perception of who you think you are.

Before you begin your training in public speaking, we need to spend a few moments examining one of our most common fears—the fear of giving a speech in front of a group of people. The 20 Questions on the permission list asked if you gave yourself permission to overcome your fear of speaking. No matter how you responded to these questions, you will benefit from a brief discussion of overcoming stage fright.

GIVING YOURSELF PERMISSION TO OVERCOME YOUR FEAR OF SPEAKING

A recent U.S. survey discovered that speaking before a group of people is the greatest fear we have. It outranks death, losing one's spouse, financial bankruptcy, illness, war, and snakes as the number one thing that terrifies us most.

Most people would probably agree with this survey. Very few people actively seek speaking opportunities, sneak into speech tournament competitions, or grab the microphone from the speaker at a PTA meeting and deliver an impromptu talk. Very few.

Many of us would prefer avoiding anything even resembling a public speaking event. Whenever someone is needed to introduce the bride and groom, deliver a brief sales presentation, speak at a luncheon, preside at the annual awards dinner, or even say a prayer at the family reunion, most folks disappear into the woodwork or run for the hills. The stress of speaking before an audience is great for many of us.

Three Ways We Stress Out When Speaking

There are three primary categories of stress that people report when they experience stage fright. Physical sensations make up the first category of stress that can occur when we are preparing to speak. The physical sensations can begin long before the actual day of the speech and may appear in the form of sleepless nights, an upset stomach, dizziness, and tingling in the hands and legs. During the speech itself, the physical sensations can include trembling knees, sweaty palms, light-headedness, a dry mouth, and nervous coughing. The exact physical sensations vary from person to person, of course, but almost everyone experiences some degree of physical discomfort or uneasiness when speaking in front of others.

The second category of stress includes emotional responses that can be experienced before, during, and after the speaking performance. They can include feelings of being overwhelmed, fear, loss of control, depression, panic, anxiety, helplessness, inadequacy, abandonment, shame, and anger.

The final category is the psychological responses of stress that can be experienced when delivering the speech. They include loss of memory, negative self-talk, jumbled thought patterns, nervous repetition of words or phrases, and the use of verbal pauses, such as "ah," "um," and "you know."

To complicate matters, these three categories of stress responses can and often do interact with one another to increase your level of stage fright. For instance, the physical sensations of trembling knees can give rise to feelings of being out of control and feeling helpless or terrified. These feelings, in turn, can cause a psychological block so the words of your talk are lost.

Sound like fun? Well, before you throw this book in the garbage and swear that you would rather hide away in some cave in Tibet than risk these terrible ills, hold on. It's not all that bad.

Even skilled speakers experience some of these responses when addressing an audience. But the difference between you and them is that they understand the speaking process. They understand that such responses are natural. It's all part of being human. They realize that these responses can be altered and changed. These speakers have prepared and practiced their speeches, and when they do experience one of these sensations of stage fright, they know how to bring themselves back under control. They know the skills and techniques to get themselves to breathe gently, center their focus of attention, and return to their talk. This chapter is designed to enable you to do the same. But first, let's look at why you are so nervous.

WHY ARE YOU SO NERVOUS?

Before you can overcome a problem, you must admit there is a problem and then understand the reasons for its existence. Most people, when confronted with a fear or anxiety, either deny its existence or fail to adequately investigate the reasons for its existence.

As to the first issue of denial, very few novice speakers are grandiose enough to boast that they have no fears regarding public speaking. Without exception, most beginning speakers are very conscious and aware of their fears, but they don't seem to know why they are afraid.

One mystified speaker angrily lamented, "Why am I so frightened? I know how to talk."

"My friends all tell me I am witty," another complained, "but when I get up to speak in front of a group, I just go blank."

And one executive grumbled, "I've had this speech written out for nearly a month, but as soon as I stand up before my audience, my eyes get blurry and my brain turns to mush. I just don't understand why."

Why, they ask.

Why is it so difficult to just talk in front of a small group of 10 or 12 people, many of whom you may know? Why is it so hard to deliver a talk when you've been talking all your life? Why is it so demanding to speak, even when you're prepared ahead of time? Why should you be so nervous?

Only One of Me and Lots of Them

Let's look at the same public speaking scene, without the sound. There is a group of people seated in a room, all facing one direction. Then one of them stands, walks to the front of the room, turns, and faces the other people, who are still seated. As she stands above the seated audience, the speaker's mouth begins to move, and her hands gesture occasionally. All eyes are on her. She looks at the group. Her mouth is moving. Their mouths are shut. She gestures. They do not. Her mouth stops moving.

The seated members clap their hands. She turns and walks down from the podium, finds her chair, and sits down. Now, everyone in the group is seated again.

What just happened? Well, if you simply watched the event and did not analyze the content of the speech, you would discover a very striking thing. The speaker becomes separate from the people she is talking to. She is no longer just one of them. Instead, she is in front of them. She is standing above them, while they are seated below. She is talking, while they are silent. She is moving and animated, while they sit motionless. She is glancing at individual members, while every eye in the audience is on her. In fact, she now controls the event, while they have little or no control. She determines the ebb and flow of the experience, while they watch for her cues. When she finishes, they applaud. She walks back down to find her chair, while they are seated and are still clapping. In short, the speaker becomes the leader of the group, and the audience become her followers.

Now, if you are the president of the United States or the conductor of the New York Philharmonic Orchestra, such an experience in front of all those people would not be frightening (maybe). Having all those eyes riveted to you, watching your every move, listening to your every word. You, the center of attention. It might not be too frightening, if you're trained for such experiences.

PUBLIC SPEAKING IS DIFFERENT FROM CONVERSATION

The fact that you've talked in conversations all your life doesn't help now. The fact that you are witty doesn't help now. The fact that you've written the speech beforehand doesn't help now. All these things don't help now because you're not involved in conversational skills.

You are involved in presentational skills. You are, in short, presenting yourself, both body and mind, to a group of people who are watching your presentation. You are no longer one of them. You are separate from them. You are presenting. They are observing. That's why it's so frightening to speak in front of an audience. No one has ever told you what to do in this situation. Sure, you've spent your entire lifetime learning how to carry on a conversation, how to informally talk to others in small group settings or at intimate gatherings at quaint restaurants, but never in your life have you been trained to present yourself to a group of people. So, remember to give yourself permission to be gentle on yourself as you learn to be different from "the rest of them"—your audience.

Public speaking is an activity that involves mental and physical presentation skills that are different from social conversational skills. To be an effective public speaker requires physical coordination, mental concentration, content organization, skills practice, and a great deal of experience. Just as it would be foolish to thrust a beginning surfer into large waves her first time out, it would be equally foolish to expect the beginning speaker to be cool, calm, and collected the first time before an audience. Formal presentation skills require as much, if not more, practice and skills improvement as surfing, or any physical sport for that matter.

There are many books and teachers who sincerely believe if a novice speaker could just relax, she would decrease her stage fright and would thus become a better public speaker. Positive thinking, self pep talks, creative visualization, and self-hypnosis are often encouraged as means of improving your speaking skills. There is some research to support such claims, but there are no shortcuts to learning these formal presentational skills, other than actually doing them.

Without the practical experience, there can be little behavioral change. You can visualize, think, and dream all you want that you can ride a surfboard. But it's the practical, hands-on experience that enables you to paddle out, stroke just enough to match the speed of the wave, stand up, and maintain a trim position as you ride the swell onto the beach.

That's what we'll be doing. Learning not only the whys, but equally important, the hows. We'll learn step-by-step how to do everything from walking up to the podium to sitting back in your chair.

SOME ENCOURAGING WORDS
ABOUT STAGE FRIGHT

Now that you know some differences between public speaking and conversation, let's conclude this chapter with some encouraging words about stage fright.

It's Natural to Be Anxious

The human body reacts to any perceived threat with certain physical, psychological, and emotional responses. If your body didn't, that would be cause for serious concern. It's natural to feel some anxiety and fear as you face an audience.

You Are Not Alone

Everyone experiences some degree of stage fright before, during, and even after a speech. There is not one person in your audience who would not feel some degree of stage fright if she were in your place, so take heart. You are not alone. We're all in this together.

You Appear Much More Relaxed Than You Feel

When speakers view a video playback of a speech, they are all, with very few exceptions, surprised at how relaxed they appear on the monitor. Feedback from audience members immediately after the talk confirms this interesting phenomenon. The speaker experiences a great deal more internal anxiety than she exhibits externally to others. You may feel really nervous on the inside, but chances are you don't appear nervous to your audience.

Have Something Important to Say

Abraham Lincoln once stated, "I shall never be old enough to speak without embarrassment when I have nothing to say." Those words still ring true today. If you feel strongly about what you are going to share with your audience, you are less likely to be fearful of them. Speak only when you have something important to say. That's an essential rule of thumb for public speaking, as well as in your daily life.

Concentrate on What Is Said

Be more concerned with the main idea you are going to share with your audience than the exact wording of your message. Don't get fixated on the details of your talk. Instead, focus your concentration on the main idea of the speech. Keep looking at the big picture, not the minutiae.

Practice Your Speech

There are very few speakers who can give well-developed speeches in an impromptu fashion, with no prior practice. Practice is one of the most important factors in confident speaking for speakers at all levels of experience. There is no substitute for actually practicing your speech in a standing position. Remember, public speaking is a physical skill, as well as an intellectual, psychological skill.

Release Your Tension before You Speak

Some speakers jog in the morning before giving a speech. Others talk nervously about their anxiety to a friend the night before. There is a television news anchor in New York who goes through five minutes of light stretching exercises in her dressing room before she goes on camera. Systematic relaxation exercises work for others, while other speakers prefer to simply pace backstage before they deliver their speech. One of the most effective relaxation exercises is to simply breathe deeply from your stomach. Keep your eyes open, but don't fix your gaze at any one thing. Just breathe deeply, evenly. You'll discover that your entire bodily rhythms will become more calm and centered. Experiment to discover what works best for you. It's your life.

Experience Reduces Anxiety

The more experience you have speaking, the less likely you are to be frightened by your next speech. It's like that with most things. The more you do it, the less frightening it is. There once was a man named Clay in the Central California farmlands who flew a crop duster, an airplane used to spray insecticides on the strawberry fields. Day after day Clay would make that old red plane loop, spin, twirl, and zip over those strawberry fields. When asked if flying like that ever frightened him, he responded, "At first it did, but after 27 years of flying a duster, I've sorta gotten used to it." The same holds true for speaking.

The Audience Is on Your Side

Think of your own reactions when you've been an audience member. Did you want the speaker to fail? To look like a fool? Most likely not. The vast majority of us want the speaker to succeed. We want the speaker to be interesting, informative, stimulating, and entertaining. The last thing we want is for the speaker to fail in her attempts to communicate. Audiences really are empathic, encouraging, and supportive, if given half a chance. One of the most uplifting thoughts you can have as you face an audience is the belief that they wish you well and they want you to succeed. They really are on your side.

WILL I EVER GET RID OF THESE BUTTERFLIES?

We've talked about giving yourself permission to make mistakes and to overcome your fears, and still you're probably wondering, "Will I ever get rid of the butterflies once and for all?" Well, there's a well-known story about a 60-year-old woman who was enrolled in a public speaking class at a local college. On the night she was scheduled to deliver her first speech, she was overcome with terror at the prospect of talking in front of all those people. She couldn't bring herself to walk up to the front of the class when her name was called, so the instructor walked over to her and asked her how she felt.

The woman replied, "I'm scared. My stomach is filled with butter-flies, and they're flying around chaotically." With some gentle encour-agement from the teacher and students, the woman slowly walked to the front of the class and spoke to the group.

The following summer, that same woman was at a family gathering. During dinner the woman's granddaughter asked, "Grandma, Daddy said you took a speech class and learned how to talk. He said you had butterflies in your stomach. Did you finally get rid of them?"

"No, I didn't get rid of those butterflies," the woman replied proudly, "but at least now they fly in formation."

Carl Jung wisely observed, "We rarely solve life's biggest problems. We merely outgrow them."[1] In your life journey, you will outgrow many of the fears and problems you are struggling with today. Your butterflies will most likely always accompany you when you speak in public, but they will be flying in formation.

ADVENTURE AND GROWTH, NOT SAFETY

A ship in a harbor is safe,
But that's not what ships were built for.

Zen saying

Many people run from new opportunities, especially if those experiences involve thinking differently, behaving differently, and feeling differently. Most of us suffer needlessly because we fear the unknown. We would rather resign ourselves to a situation that is painful because it is also familiar, predictable, and in some ways safe, rather than venture into the unknown. But perhaps we were intended to explore the unknown in our life's voyage.

For most of us, learning how to speak in front of others involves ven-turing out into the unknown. We are like ships in a harbor, not really comfortable with the prospects of setting sail into open sea, because every voyage requires some element of risk, and maybe change. But that's what learning is all about—to change, to improve, to be freer than you were before.

Just keep in mind that the purpose of life is not to be perfect. It's to try new things as we grow older. To learn more about this world, our friends, and ourselves. We should learn to discover and communicate what we think, how we feel, and who we are as we journey during our lifetime.

Now it's time to leave the harbor.

COMMUNICATION ACTIVITIES

Personal Activities

1. **Giving yourself permission**

   Review your responses to the 20 statements in the permission list. Select one item that you did not agree with. Read the statement aloud five times in a definite, confident voice. Close your eyes and imagine you are actually experiencing the situation described in the statement. For example, "I give myself permission to not know all the answers." Imagine being asked a question by a teacher and simply responding, "I don't know." Imagine feeling comfortable with your response. Imagine the teacher smiling and saying, "That's okay. I don't know the answer either." Imagine that you and the teacher both begin to laugh. How did that feel to you? Try another permission statement if you had more than one "no" response.

2. **A different cultural perspective**

   Ask an individual from a different cultural background about his or her attitudes and feelings about the permission list presented in this chapter. How does his or her culture perceive the ideas raised by the statements in the permission list? How do you feel about his or her responses?

3. **Imagining the worst**

   Imagine you are delivering a five-minute speech about programming a VCR to a group of 25 high school seniors. Halfway through your speech, you draw a blank—you can't remember what you were going to say. What is the worst thing (or things) that could happen? Be specific. Make a list of all the horrors that could happen. Look at your list. How would you respond to each of the items on your list? Be strong. Be assertive. Tell those high school seniors a thing or two. Did any of the audience members come to your rescue? How do you feel? Was it all that bad?

Class Activities

1. **Receiving permission**

   Pair up with another student in class and take turns granting one another permission on the statements from the permission list. If you responded "no" to any statement on your list, have your partner grant you permission to do that behavior. For instance, have your partner tell you in a firm and definite tone of voice, "I (partner) give you permission to make mistakes!" Ask her to say the statement three or four times. How did it feel? What did you think? After your partner has repeated this process with three or four other statements you disagreed with, switch roles and give your partner permission statements. Be prepared to share your reactions to this assignment in class.

2. **Group sharing: Letting others know what you fear**

The class is to be divided into groups of five students each. Each student is to share three or four things he or she fears. As each individual shares a specific fear, other students in the group can raise their hands to indicate that they too share that same fear. You'll be surprised at how many others share not only your fear of public speaking, but other physical, psychological, and emotional fears as well. You are not alone. The group can also discuss how they cope or deal with these fears.

3. **You appear more relaxed than you feel**

This exercise will be videotaped in your class. Give an informal 30-second talk about your public speaking fears. You can share anything you'd like during this brief talk. After the entire class has spoken, view the presentations *without* sound. What did you look like? Did you look as anxious or frightened as you felt? How did the other students appear while they were speaking? Discuss your responses to this activity in class.

4. **Worst nightmare speech**

Make a list of the five most terrible things an audience could do to you while you're speaking—throw paper, walk out of the room, shout criticism, sleep, "boo" and "hiss," or laugh. This will be like your worst nightmare. But, you'll discover, it's not that bad. Assign members of the class to role-play your "terrible" behaviors while you are speaking. Give an informal 30-second talk about a happy childhood memory and let the students act out their roles (the horrible behaviors). How was it? Was the experience as bad as you thought it would be? Did you laugh? Did the audience laugh? What feelings do you have? How did the exercise change your attitude toward speaking? Be prepared to discuss your reactions to this assignment in class.

NOTE

1. Carl J. Jung, *The Symbolic Life* (Princeton, NJ: Princeton University Press, 1950).

3

GIVING YOUR FIRST SPEECH
Beginning Your Journey

The eight young children huddled together as they watched their swimming instructor dive effortlessly into the water and surface right before their feet at the edge of the pool. It was their first morning of beginning swimming lessons.

"Okay, everyone, lay your towels on the bench and get into the shallow end of the pool," the swim teacher ordered with a smile.

"Do we have to?" complained one five-year-old boy. "It's too scary," shouted another. None of the eight beginners moved. And then, all of a sudden, one skinny boy burst into tears and ran for his mother at the far end of the pool. The instructor quickly hopped out of the water and walked over to the crying boy as the other seven children clutched their towels and watched.

Leticia kneeled beside her crying student and smiled to the mother. "Hold my hand, Simon," Leticia offered in a gentle, soothing voice. "The water is pretty warm, and I'll be right by your side."

"I don't want to get wet yet," protested Simon.

"You'll like the water once you get in," assured Leticia, still kneeling by his side.

Simon remained silent as Leticia slowly reached for his hand. "You'll like the water—it's warm," she whispered once more as he slowly let go of his mother's hand. Leticia took his hand and walked Simon to the steps. The next moment, they both entered the water together as the seven others stood looking on. The water was warm and he smiled as he cautiously inched deeper into the pool. This was Simon's first swimming lesson. His journey was beginning.

There are many firsts during a lifetime. The first swimming lesson. The first car. The first date. The first time we leave home. Each experience is characterized by both excitement and some degree of anxiety over the unknown. What will it be like? How will I do? What will I feel? These and many other questions confront us as we get closer to the event. And if you're normal, many times you feel like Simon and say to yourself, "I don't want to get wet yet." But once you're in the water, you realize that many of your fears were unfounded and the new experience was worth the risk.

YOUR FIRST SPEECH

"I don't want to give a speech yet!" "Do I have to?" "It's too scary!" are common reactions to the first oral assignment in any public speaking class. Yet, public speaking is a lot like learning to swim. The only way you can learn to swim is by getting wet. And the only way you can learn to speak is by getting up in front of the audience and speaking. You really get a feel for speaking only by speaking. Not by learning to research. Not by outlining speeches. And not by constructing beautiful visual aids, although we will learn how to do these and many other skills later in this book. But for now, your journey begins by getting up and speaking.

Your public speaking instructor will most likely assign a simple speech during the first week or two of class just to get you used to the water—to actually have you begin your journey as a public speaker. This chapter is intended to get you prepared for that first speech.

Let's start by discovering what public speaking is.

PUBLIC SPEAKING

Public speaking is defined as speaking before an audience. There are three primary purposes for giving speeches: to inform, to persuade, or to entertain. College lectures, a winery tour, and a demonstration of flower arranging are speeches that primarily inform. Persuasive speaking includes a fund-raising talk for the Asian Club on campus, a speech advocating blood donation, and a sales presentation for the latest computer. After-dinner speaking and comedy club acts are examples of speeches to entertain. Usually speeches are technically a combination of all three, but the primary goal of a given speech is to inform, to persuade, or to entertain.

FOUR SPEAKING METHODS

In addition to the three general purposes of public speaking, there are different styles or methods of delivering a speech. The four basic speaking methods or approaches are manuscript, memorized, impromptu, and extemporaneous.

Manuscript Delivery Method

The manuscript delivery method consists of reading a speech from a text or manuscript. The speech is written word for word, and the speaker does not stray from the prepared text as she reads to the audience.

One advantage of this delivery method is that the content of the speech is guaranteed as long as the speaker sticks to the text. This could be important if the exact wording of a speech is vital, as in scientific presentations or political addresses.

There are many disadvantages to this style of speaking. The obvious disadvantage to manuscript delivery is the lack of natural, spontaneous delivery on the part of the speaker. Eye contact is decreased, because most speakers using this method read the entire speech, word for word, instead of establishing eye contact with their audience. Animated gestures, facial expressions, and body movement are limited by this style of speaking. Spontaneous speaker response to audience feedback is not easily attained with this delivery method, as the text is already determined. We've all known professors who relied on this style of lecturing, semester after semester, year after year.

Memorized Delivery Method

The second method of speaking delivery is memorized. In this style, the speaker memorizes the text of a speech, word for word, and then recites the speech without the use of the manuscript.

One advantage of the memorized delivery method is the speaker is now able to look at her audience more, since the manuscript is no longer in front of her. The speaker is also more spontaneous in her gestures and body movement. This method is utilized by actors and Disneyland tour guides, to name a few.

The disadvantages of this method are many. Unless you are gifted at memorization, it's difficult to commit to memory even the briefest of talks. Memorization requires a great deal of time and effort, even for the best of speakers. To make matters worse, once you've gotten the speech memorized, you face the prospect of forgetting a part of the speech when you're speaking.

Once the speaker forgets just one word, everything that followed that particular word is out the window. Swooosh…into the universe, never to be seen again. The speaker usually goes blank. And that's one of the most pitiful looks you can ever see on a human being—just *blank*. Don't let this happen to you.

Impromptu Delivery Method

Impromptu speaking consists of speaking to an audience on the spur of the moment, without prior preparation or practice. Most public speaking nightmares involve sadistic variations on this style of speaking, with hundreds of shrieking demons dancing around you, as you stand on the stage, naked, struggling to find words, any words, to begin your talk. (Wow, what did we eat before we went to bed last night?)

Doesn't sound like there's anything good or of redeeming value about impromptu speaking. But nothing could be further from the truth. Once mastered, impromptu speaking can change the way you see yourself and how you communicate with others. The confidence you receive from being skilled in impromptu speaking can literally change your self-concept.

Extemporaneous Delivery Method

Of the four methods of speaking, the extemporaneous method is perhaps the best style for most public presentations, because it utilizes the best aspects of the other three, while balancing their respective weaknesses. Extemporaneous speaking is speaking that is prepared and practiced ahead of time, but the exact wording isn't determined until the speaker delivers the speech.

The speech is researched and outlined ahead of time. Normally, the outline contains only 25–30 percent of the total words that will be delivered in the speech. Usually full-sentence outline structure is used, with an introduction, a body, and a conclusion. This outline is the skeleton of the speech, and the meat of the talk; the other 70–75 percent of the wording isn't exactly determined until the speaker delivers the speech.

Practice is another requirement for extemporaneous speaking. Once the speech is researched and outlined, the speaker practices the speech, first with the outline, then with only note cards. Many extemporaneous speakers deliver their entire speeches from only one or two 4 x 6-inch note cards containing a brief key-word outline of points.

The speech should be practiced at least five to seven times in its entirety. Too little practice doesn't provide the command of the main points of the talk and the general flow of the speech. Too much practice increases the probability the speech will begin to sound memorized. You need to balance the two extremes as far as practice is concerned. Balance in speech practice, as in life.

Once the speech has been prepared and practiced, the speaker is ready to deliver the speech. The primary advantage of this style is that the speaker is organized and knows what points need to be covered, much like the manuscript and memorized speaking methods, but without the loss of natural delivery and the threat of forgetting any one of hundreds of words contained in the talk. Furthermore, the speaker has the spontaneity of impromptu speaking, without the added burden of having to construct the speech while standing in front of the audience. The extemporaneous delivery method is the style you will most likely use in your public speaking class.

YOUR MESSAGE

No matter which of the four speaking methods you use, the message of your speech is the most important element of the entire public speaking process. Without a message, there is no reason for the speech. And for that matter, there is no reason for you, the speaker. The delivery of the speaker can be dynamic and the organization of the speech can be flawless, but without a relevant topic, the speaker is simply wasting the audience's time and his or her own as well.

For your first speaking assignment, you may be asked to introduce a classmate or yourself, share an achievement from your life, describe a turning point, or support a belief or opinion. No matter what you are asked to speak on, here are three things you should consider when developing your message—the speaking situation, the audience, and the topic.

The Speaking Situation

The first question to ask yourself is what is the speaking situation? What are the requirements of this assignment? What is the general goal of this speech—to inform, to persuade, or to entertain? What is the specific purpose of this speech—to introduce yourself, describe an achievement, or support a belief? What is the time limit for the speech? Are any note cards permitted? Can I bring visual aids? When is my speaking day? Am I required to dress up for this presentation? And is there a makeup speech policy in case I'm unable to give my speech? Hey, no wimping out!

The Audience

The second question you must ask yourself is who is my audience? For this class assignment, you will most likely be speaking to other students. In the future, however, you may be required to speak to a variety of audiences, such as a gathering of business clients, a city council, a neighborhood watch group, or a political rally. For these groups, a more thorough analysis of your audience will be required. A more in-depth discussion of audience analysis will be presented in Chapter 4.

For your first speech, however, here are some basic questions you might consider: What is the gender makeup of the class? What is the average age of my listeners? Are most of the students undeclared majors, from a variety of majors, or primarily communication studies majors? And what are the cultural backgrounds of my audience? The answer to these and related questions about your classmates will enable you to be more aware of and sensitive to your audience. For instance, if your audience is primarily female, you might want to use examples or illustrations that relate to women. Or if your audience is mostly freshmen with undeclared majors, your speech should be designed with them in mind. Remember who you're speaking to.

The Topic (Your Message)

The topic of your first speech will be determined to a great extent by the nature of the assignment. A speech of introduction will focus on your speaking partner or yourself. An achievement speech will require you to share an award, honor, or goal you have realized. And a speech of definition will concentrate on a specific word, term, or concept. Whatever the specific assignment is, however, you must make sure your topic is specific, relevant to your audience, and interesting. Your topic should be specific enough to be covered within the given time limits. Speak about a solar eclipse, rather than the entire universe. Limit your speech to only three aspects of your speaking partner, rather than 15. Your topic should be relevant to your audience, so keep them in mind when you select your topic. And finally, your topic should be interesting to both you and your audience. This is not the time to present a topic of common knowledge. Share something new, unique, or unusual.

In Chapter 4, we will explore the brainstorming technique for generating speech topics and selecting main points. But for this first speech, your topic should be specific, relevant to your audience, and interesting.

Take these questions seriously, whether you're introducing your speaking partner, relating a story, or explaining a concept. Your classmates will hear you speak for only a few minutes in the next week or two, so make it worth their time.

YOUR SPEECH ORGANIZATION

One of the most important skills you will learn in your public speaking class is how to organize a speech. Although there are many ways to organize a speech, we will use the traditional introduction, body, and conclusion pattern. Here is a brief introduction to the three basic components of a speech. We will discuss them in more detail when we get to Chapter 6.

The Introduction

The first few seconds of any speech are critical in establishing its rhythm and mood. Therefore, your introduction is very important to the successful reception of your talk. Don't begin your speech with "Ah, my name is…," "I'm going to be talking about…," or "Wow, it's scary up here." Instead, every introduction should accomplish two goals:

Get the audience's attention.   The first words from your mouth should be your attention getter. An attention getter can be an audience question, a startling statistic, a thought-provoking quotation, or an appropriate joke.

Preview of main points.   The preview of main points should follow your attention getter. This is simply a one-sentence statement of the two or three main points you will present in your speech. "Today, I'd like to share three things about my speaking partner, Jill." "For the next few minutes, I want to discuss three aspects of love." Or "This morning I'm going to share the turning point of my life and the lesson I learned from it." Your preview of main points is intended to focus the attention of your audience on your topic and give them an idea of the main points you will be addressing.

The Body

The body of your speech develops the main points of your talk. It constitutes about 75–85 percent of your speech. It is in the body of your speech that you present the majority of your information. Any speech, regardless of length, should contain only three or four main points. More than four main points will likely confuse or lose your audience. Here are three easy ways to organize the main points of your speech.

Topical order.   Many times a speech topic will lend itself to a natural division of points. If you are introducing your speaking partner to the class, you might want to share three of her personality characteristics— intelligence, humor, and kindness. Or if you're explaining reasons to shop locally, you might discuss the three points of supporting local business, making friends, and saving transportation costs.

Chronological order.   Time order is another way you can arrange your main points in the body of a speech. Often speeches unfold in terms of past, present, and future. In a speech of introduction, you could share a highlight from your past, your present job, and finally, a professional goal you want to accomplish in the future.

Spatial order.   A third way to arrange the main points of your speech is spatial order. You could discuss a building in terms of basement, main floor, and attic. Or you might describe California in terms of seashore, Central Valley, and the Sierra Nevada Mountains.

No matter what main-point order you use for your first speech, the use of *numbered transitions* will be helpful in signposting and guiding your audience through your talk. A numbered transition leads the audience from one point to another. "The first thing I want to share with you about Marcus is...," "The second characteristic of love is...," "The final reason for shopping locally is..." Help your audience listen to and remember what you're talking about by using numbered transitions in the body of your speech.

The Conclusion

The manner in which you conclude your speech is every bit as important as how you began your talk. Often, a novice speaker will simply conclude by muttering, "Well, I guess that's all," or ask, "Are there any questions?" But not you! You'll end your first speech skillfully.

Review the main points.   Begin your conclusion by summarizing the main points of your speech in a one-sentence statement. "Today, I've talked about Jill's intelligence, humor, and kindness," or "This morning I've briefly described California's seashore, Central Valley, and the Sierra Nevada Mountains." Remember, just a one-sentence summary.

Final thought.   After you've reviewed the main points of your speech, you'll want to leave your audience with something to remember. Here are four easy ways to conclude your speech. First, a short quotation is a good way to end your speech with words your audience can remember. Second, a brief anecdote can be shared to illustrate your point. Third, a goodwill wish can plant a seed in the minds of your listeners—"I hope that you will all experience deep friendships in your lifetime." And finally, a call to action is a powerful way to end your speech—"I want you all to introduce yourselves to Marcus this semester and get to know a friendly man."

YOUR DELIVERY

By now, you have a clear idea of what the message of your first speech will be and how to organize your message into an introduction, body, and conclusion. The third topic we will explore in preparation for this first speech is your delivery. Delivery is how you present your speech to your audience. In Chapter 7, we will examine speaker delivery in greater detail, but for now, we'll introduce three basic elements of delivery— your body, your face and eyes, and your voice.

Your Body

Your speech begins as soon as the audience realizes you are the speaker. So, as you walk up to the podium, keep in mind that your audience is already making judgments about you. Walk up to the podium slowly, deliberately. Don't rush up to the front of the class. Some speakers prefer using a podium, while others like to stand by its side or stand in front of it altogether. Whatever you feel most comfortable with, get set before you begin speaking. Balance your posture by spreading your feet about shoulder-width apart and keeping your posture straight. Look at your audience, smile, and then take a deep breath or two before you begin your speech.

During the speech, remember to gesture naturally. Don't fold your arms, hold them behind your back, or put your hands in your pockets. Natural and appropriate gestures can add life to your speech.

Your body movement should be natural and expressive. The worst thing you could do is hide motionless behind the podium like a statue. The second worst thing you could do is pace the floor like a caged animal. Moderation is the key. Something in between no body movement and repetitive body movement. Use your body when you're telling a story. Try walking a few steps when you're stating a numbered transition in the body of your speech. Let the audience see your body communicate your message, as well as hear your words.

Your Face and Eyes

It's amazing how your face is capable of communicating messages without words. A smile, a raised eyebrow, a frown, a stare, and a downcast glance can communicate powerful messages without one word being uttered. During your speech, your face and eyes will be the primary visual focus of attention for your audience. Use your facial expressions and eye contact to reinforce your verbal messages.

During your speech, look at individuals in the audience. Don't stare at the floor, your notes, or the back wall. You can do that all you want when you get home after you've given your speech. But for now, when you're speaking to your audience, acknowledge them by seeing them. And remember to use facial expressions to reinforce the points you are attempting to make.

Your Voice

Use an enlarged conversational tone of voice when speaking to your audience. A common belief of beginning speakers is that they have to sound like a television announcer or political orator to be effective. The secret is not to sound or be like someone else, but rather, to sound like and be yourself. Talk to your audience in an enlarged conversational tone of voice, so you can be heard in the back of the room. Speak as if you were talking to family or friends, but loud enough so everyone can hear.

And remember to breathe. How you breathe will determine how you speak. Holding your breath or not breathing deeply will tire and strain your voice. Breathe deeply. Even before you begin your speech, take a few deep breaths. Between sentences, consciously pause and breathe. Take your time. Don't rush yourself. The audience will welcome your pauses. The silence gives your audience time to digest your words and provides you with a moment to breathe.

Add life to your voice by varying your rate of speech, your volume, and your pitch. Don't speak in a monotone voice. Be more like a roller coaster than a train by adding variety to your rate, volume, and pitch. Communicate your desire to speak by being enthusiastic! This is the only time your audience will get to listen to you during the next week or two, so give them all you've got—speak with enthusiasm.

HELPFUL HINTS FOR YOUR FIRST SPEECH

Now you know the topic for the first speech, how to organize it, and how to deliver your talk in an enthusiastic manner. Here are some helpful hints that will ensure your success:

First, *prepare ahead of time.* Don't wait until the last minute to begin your preparation and practice. Give yourself plenty of time. Speaking is a process that takes time. You can't take a microwave approach to this journey. It's more like a crockpot or a roast in the oven. Be spacious with yourself. Begin preparing your speech as soon as it is assigned.

Second, *don't write a manuscript* for your speech. The immediate response to the first assignment is to write the speech out word for word. A manuscript makes you feel safe, in control. But in reality, just the opposite is true. A manuscript forces you to memorize, and that's far more involved and difficult than simply speaking from an outline or note card.

Third, *practice your entire speech* at least five times from a standing position. A common mistake is to practice the speech silently at a stoplight or in the room before class begins. You need to begin practicing two or three days before you're scheduled to speak. Practice in a standing position. Work on your introduction first, until you feel you've mastered it. Then move to the first main point of the body. Practice the first point until you have it down. Once you're familiar and comfortable with every part of your speech, practice your speech in its entirety. Time your speech. Add or delete material to meet the time limits. Practice your speech again. After five complete speech practices, you should be ready for your audience. Take your responsibilities seriously, and honor your commitments to others and yourself.

Fourth, *keep your speech in perspective.* This first speech is not your life. It's just one assignment, in one class. In the light of eternity, it's not a big deal. Your relationships with family and friends, your personal integrity, your emotional and physical health, your happiness, and countless other facets of life are far more significant.

Finally, *be gentle on yourself.* Give yourself permission to make mistakes, to not be perfect, to be human. The purpose of this assignment is not to be perfect, but to make progress, to learn new skills and behaviors. Progress, not perfection! So be spacious with yourself. Give yourself plenty of room to learn and to grow.

COMMUNICATION ACTIVITIES

Personal Activities

1. **Reflecting on an earlier success**

   Think back on a time when you learned a new skill such as riding a bike, skiing, dancing, or driving a car. What were your thoughts and feelings before you learned that skill? What were the steps you took to learn that skill? To eventually master the skill? What were your thoughts and feelings after you became proficient in that skill? What did you learn about your ability to learn? How can this learning apply to your first public speaking experience?

2. **Mad, glad, and sad**

   Divide a sheet of paper into thirds. Label the columns *mad, glad,* and *sad.* Spend the next five minutes thinking of things that make you mad, glad, or sad. Write each item in the appropriate column. After a few minutes you'll discover you've made quite a list. Congratulations! You've just created your first list of speech topics. Not every item you listed will be appropriate for your speech class, but a few of them might be. Consider using some of these topics for future speech assignments. It's always good to speak about something you feel passionate about, and your list will surely give you some fine ideas.

3. **Talking to three empty chairs**

   Go to the largest room in your home and arrange three empty chairs in a row facing you. The chairs should be five feet apart. Imagine there is a person in each one of the chairs. Simply stand in front of the chairs for a few minutes. Then talk about whatever comes into your mind. Have fun with this exercise. How did it feel to you? Did your delivery become more animated as you went along? Did you ham it up at all? What was this like for you?

Class Activities

1. **Small group sharing: Helping a sixth grader give a speech**

   Divide the class into groups of five or six. One of the students in each group is to role-play a sixth-grade student who has to give a three-minute speech of self-introduction to his class in one week. The sixth-grade student (role-player) doesn't know anything about public speaking and has asked your group for help. The other group members are to share whatever information they can remember from this chapter in an attempt to help the young speaker.

2. **Personal growth speech**

   Think of some old behavior, habit, or belief that used to cause you discomfort, frustration, or pain. Maybe things like procrastination, overeating, being a poor listener, or having a victim's attitude. Present a one-minute speech on your process of personal growth that led to overcoming this particular behavior, habit, or belief. Begin your speech with an audience question and conclude with a final thought.

3. **Future goal speech**

   Select one specific personal goal, dream, or aspiration you'd like to accomplish during your lifetime. It can be a physical goal, such as participating in a triathlon or learning to ski. It can be a professional goal, such as becoming a career counselor or writing a book. Or it can be a spiritual goal, like learning to meditate or deepening your prayer life. Present a one-minute speech describing your goal and why you are seeking it. Begin with an audience question and conclude with a final thought.

4. **Speech of self-introduction**

   Prepare, practice, and deliver a three-minute speech introducing yourself to the class. The speech will contain an introduction, a body with three main points, and a conclusion. Each main point should describe a personality characteristic, achievement, hobby, interest, or goal. Try to develop your points with stories, illustrations, examples, quotations, and definitions. Your introduction should contain a brief attention getter and preview of points. Your conclusion should contain a review of points and a final thought.

5. **Speech of introduction**

   Prepare, practice, and deliver a three-minute speech introducing your speaking partner to the class. Spend 30 minutes interviewing your speaking partner. The speech will contain an introduction, a body with three main points, and a conclusion. Each main point should describe a personality characteristic, achievement, hobby, interest, or goal. Try to develop your points with stories, illustrations, examples, quotations, and definitions. Your introduction should contain a brief attention getter and preview of points. Your conclusion should contain a review of points and a final thought.

4

SELECTING YOUR TOPIC
Choosing Your Path

It was getting dark outside and the professor was preparing to leave her office when she heard the knock on the door

"Come on in," the professor said as she stood up to greet her visitor.

"I'm sorry to bother you this late, but I'm in trouble," the student said softly as he entered.

"Tell me about it," the woman said as she offered her student a chair.

"Well, I'm scheduled to give my speech tomorrow morning, and I've had a hard time deciding what to talk on. There were just so many topics to speak on," he complained, "that I couldn't decide."

"That must be a terrible feeling," remarked the professor.

"Can I do my speech next week?" he asked.

"No," she replied gently.

"Well, what am I supposed to do?" he blurted out, looking her in the eyes for the first time.

"You've had three weeks to decide on a topic and work on the speech. Now you have less than 24 hours. What do you want to do with your situation?" she inquired.

"I'd like to drop the class, but I can't. I need it to graduate. I guess I'll just have to give the speech on something," he sighed.

"How would you like me to help you with this?" the professor asked.

"Oh, I'll just do it myself," he muttered to himself in frustration as he walked out of the office and into the night.

IT'S YOUR CHOICE

Whether your speech is for a public speaking class, a sales presentation, an awards dinner, or a retirement roast, you will rarely be assigned a specific speech topic. It is more likely that you will be given a great deal of freedom and latitude in your selection of a speech topic.

On the surface, this may sound desirable. But it often presents the beginning speaker with one of the most challenging tasks in the public speaking process—the sole responsibility to choose, from the hundreds of thousands of possible subjects, one topic to speak on.

Sound easy? Maybe not. Many experienced speakers report this is the most difficult part of speech making—simply choosing something to talk about. Individuals experiencing difficulty at this point complain there are either "too many topics" or "not enough." But no matter which of these two predicaments they find themselves in, they do not choose a topic.

That is where the trouble begins.

We're not going to examine the many possible psychological and emotional reasons why individuals have difficulty deciding on speech topics, or anything else for that matter. It is apparent that indecision, and the immobility that follows, hampers many of us in our daily lives. Should I marry or not? Should I date this person or not? Should I leave the job or not? Should I stay in school or not? And the list goes on and on.

Indecision is something we must contend with in our daily lives, as well as in the speech-making process. But remember that indecision is a decision in and of itself—the decision not to decide. And that's okay. Many people spend a great deal of their lives not deciding.

But that will not work for your public speaking life. You must decide on a specific topic before you can begin preparing for your talk. In this chapter, we examine the five steps involved in selecting your topic and choosing the main points for your speech. The five steps are: brainstorming possible topics, determining your speaking purpose, determining your specific purpose, brainstorming main points, and analyzing your audience.

BRAINSTORMING POSSIBLE TOPICS

The first step is to *brainstorm* possible topics. The primary purpose in the brainstorming technique is to generate a large number of ideas without evaluation. In other words, the goal is to not judge your ideas as you write them down for consideration, but simply to collect as many ideas as possible. This technique may feel strange initially, because much of our daily energy is spent evaluating and judging the rightness and wrongness, the goodness and badness, the effectiveness and ineffectiveness of just about everything we experience.

The first task in brainstorming is to *get away to a quiet place* that is free from distractions and interruptions. You don't want friends talking, the telephone ringing, or the dog barking as you generate your list of ideas for the speech topic. Once you've secured a quiet, private place to work—such as your office, kitchen, or dining room—get a pad of paper, a pen or pencil, a kitchen timer, and a Diet Pepsi.

Set the timer for 10 minutes. The reason you need a clock is to focus your efforts for a specific period of time. Remember, "work expands to fill the time allotted," so if you're given three weeks to decide on a speech topic, you'll generally take the entire three weeks. Once the clock is set for 10 minutes, get comfortable with your pencil and pad, open the Diet Pepsi, and you're set.

The second task in brainstorming is to *get crazy* and write down anything that comes to your mind as a possible speech topic. Most people can think of one or two topics when faced with a blank sheet of paper, but get really crazy and write down *any* idea that comes to mind.

The most important requirement of this technique is to *free yourself from self-evaluation or criticism.* What will restrict and hinder you the most in selecting a speech topic is your negative response to your own suggestions and ideas. You need to give yourself permission to get a little loose and generate ideas, any ideas, no matter how wild or crazy. Let your handwriting get crazy too. Throw out all the restrictions you normally impose on yourself. As you get crazy during this second step of the brainstorming process, keep in mind the following four suggestions:

1. Don't evaluate or judge any of your ideas.
2. Quantity of ideas is desired, not quality.
3. The wilder the ideas are, the better.
4. Combine ideas to create new ones.

To give you a picture of what this process might produce, let's pretend that Yari has to speak on the topic of "public speaking." Let's see how many brainstorming topics he can generate in 10 minutes. Yari grabs a pencil, takes a last sip of Diet Pepsi, and ("click") he's off and running.

fear
notes
being a president
advantages of public speaking
uses of public speaking training

podiums
training for public speaking
talk show host
making money speaking
being a teacher

hand gestures
looking at the ceiling
power speaking
being an actor
having people look up to you

learning to think logically
being persuasive
ways public speaking can help me grow personally
being a tour guide
speech contests

speaking as a lawyer
public speaking professions
being a speech coach for the movies
being on radio
being confident

having people think I'm smart
stage fright
telling stories to others
being funny
getting a job as a sports announcer

going into advertising
giving speeches for the church
teaching people to not be afraid of audiences
being a speech tutor
sharing my feelings with others

selling cars
ways public speaking can improve my interaction with others

Buzz!!—The 10-minute alarm just went off. Pencil down, Yari! Good job! Now finish off that Diet Pepsi while we count your brainstorming topics. There are 37. A pretty productive brainstorming session. And who says there's nothing to talk about with the topic "public speaking"?

Now, you might have cheered for some of the items on his list, sneered at others, but that's your evaluating mind in action. And the first rule of brainstorming is for you *not* to evaluate any of the ideas or suggestions during this second step of the brainstorming process. Once you get the hang of not judging, the brainstorming process really takes off.

Once you've generated a massive list of possible topics, you're set for the final step of getting selective. Your final task is to *select one topic from the pile of topics.* You might want to take some time, a few hours to a couple of days, between your brainstorming session and the selection step. Your brain may need a rest after that 10-minute brainstorming session, and it's good to leave the list for a while, just to give your unconscious time to mull it over.

After you feel rested, it's time to examine your list of possible topics and select the one that you'd like to speak on. As you look over your list, cross out all those topics that you're not interested in or that might not be of interest to your particular audience. If possible, select topics you have previous experience with or knowledge of. Also, select topics you would enjoy researching.

Now Yari was set to begin this part of his task—eliminating the weak, flimsy, or unsound topics from his list. As he looked over the list, he eliminated the vast majority of brainstorming possibilities because he wasn't interested in them or he didn't possess a great deal of previous experience or knowledge of them. Yari finally selected three topics he found interesting and was willing to spend time researching. The topics were "Being a speech coach for the movies," "Ways public speaking can help me grow personally," and "Uses of public speaking training."

After a day or two, he finally decided on the topic "Uses of public speaking training" as his speech topic. That's a topic of interest to him and of possible interest to his audience (college students in the beginning speech class).

We finally have a topic for the speech! We are now in a position to determine our speaking purpose, the second step in the process.

DETERMINING YOUR SPEAKING PURPOSE

Once you've determined the topic of your speech, you must decide what effect you want your talk to have on the audience. It is important that you decide that effect because it will determine how you phrase your specific purpose statement and the selection of your main points.

As you will recall, the three purposes for speaking are to inform, persuade, and entertain. Although a speech may contain a little of each category, you will need to decide which *primary effect* your talk will have on the listeners. Will it be to inform? Persuade? Or entertain?

For the topic we've chosen, "Uses of public speaking training," we could choose any one of the three primary purposes for speaking. We could inform the audience about the uses of public speaking training. We could attempt to persuade our audience that public speaking does have many practical uses. Or we could entertain the audience by sharing humorous uses of public speaking training.

Yari chooses to inform his audience about the uses of public speaking training. He doesn't want to persuade his audience or entertain them. That's his speaking purpose—to inform. Now he's ready to go to step 3.

DETERMINING YOUR SPECIFIC PURPOSE

Now that you've decided on your speaking purpose, you must determine your specific purpose. The *specific purpose* states exactly (1) what you want to do with your audience, and (2) what you want to tell them. For instance, the specific purpose "To persuade my audience to get annual physical examinations" specifies both goals. First, it states what you want to do with the audience—"to persuade." And second, it states what you want to tell them—"to get annual physical examinations." Notice that the specific purpose is stated in the infinitive form of a verb (to…), so it clearly stipulates which of the three speaking purposes it is setting out to accomplish.

Here are some examples of specific purpose statements under their respective headings of speaking purposes.

Speaking purpose: *To inform.*

Specific purpose: To demonstrate how to change a flat tire.
                     To report the results of a recent survey.
                     To explain the art of flower arranging.

Speaking purpose: *To persuade.*

Specific purpose: To motivate my audience to jog a mile a day.
                     To persuade my audience to buy life insurance.
                     To increase my audience's willingness to vote.

Speaking purpose: *To entertain.*

Specific purpose: To amuse my audience by explaining how to pig out.
                     To amaze my audience with a demonstration of magic.

Let's return to Yari's speech topic—"Uses of public speaking training"—and put it into a specific purpose statement. Because he wants to inform his audience, he needs to state his specific purpose using the infinitive. The specific purpose becomes

"To inform the audience about the uses of public speaking training."

In the first part of the specific purpose, he specifies what it is he wants to do with the audience—*"To inform the audience."* In the second part of the specific purpose, he specifies what he wants them to know—*"about the uses of public speaking training."* After we have selected the main points of a speech, we will reword this second section of the specific purpose to reflect the actual main points we will use in the speech.

SELECTING YOUR MAIN POINTS

Now that you have your specific purpose, you need to begin brainstorming possible main points for the body of the speech. The main points are those two or three supporting thoughts or ideas you wish to present in the body of the talk. These main points make up the skeleton or structure of the speech body and provide the direction the speech will take.

A common mistake beginning speakers make at this point of the process is settling for the first two or three main points that come to mind. And they don't think of any other main points. They stop the process right there and call it quits.

This is a mistake. Your first thoughts are not always your best, and this method of selecting main points runs the risk of missing better main-point possibilities that would surface if more time and effort were devoted to this step. The first step in selecting the main points for your speech topic is to generate a large selection of points to choose from.

Brainstorming Main Points

Here again, the brainstorming technique we just learned can be extremely helpful. Instead of brainstorming possible speech topics, we use the same technique to generate possible main-point ideas for our topic. Yari can begin the brainstorming process by using the specific purpose he has selected, "To inform the audience about the uses of public speaking training."

With a second Diet Pepsi in hand, Yari has set the alarm for 10 minutes, and once again he begins the brainstorming process. But this time he's generating main points for his talk.

    improves your speaking
    get to listen to speeches
    get to meet people in class
    satisfy the oral requirement for State College
    my friend is in the class

    learn to speak up in my other classes
    become more skilled in my interpersonal interactions
    appear more attractive to the opposite sex
    my parents will be proud of my speech
    improves self-image

    learn to relax when under pressure
    improves presentational skills
    improves my oral interpretation skills

make me a better salesperson
make me more persuasive

maybe I'll get a date
learn about speaker credibility
improves effectiveness in business
my friends will want to have me teach them skills
be more effective in beating traffic tickets

get a summer job
income will go up in the years to come
people will like me
my grades will improve
my boss will like me

make me more pleasant
learn to think more quickly

Buzz!!—That's 10 minutes. Yari puts the pencil down and takes a sip of Diet Pepsi. He generated 27 items or possible uses for learning public speaking. Each item could serve as a main point that could support his topic—"The uses of public speaking training." Once again, some ideas are better than others, but the goal in brainstorming is quantity of ideas, not quality.

The next step, as in the brainstorming process for topic selection, is to examine the list and eliminate the weaker items on the basis of speaker interest, previous knowledge and experience, and possible audience interest in the main points.

Having completed the elimination process, Yari finally decides on "Improves presentational skills," "Improves effectiveness in business," and "Improves self-image." He finally arrives at the following tentative outline for his speech:

Specific Purpose: *To inform the audience about three uses of public speaking training.*

Main Points: I. Public speaking improves your presentational skills.
    II. Public speaking helps you become more effective in business.
    III. Public speaking improves your self-image.

The speech topic and main-point structure do not mysteriously appear. Their creation takes some time and effort on the part of you, the speaker. It involves the commitment to sit down by yourself and

brainstorm possible topics and main points. It requires making decisions
as to the topic and main points you are to work with for a period of time
in researching, outlining, and practicing before you present your speech.
Some people are not prepared or willing to make this commitment, like
the young man in the professor's office at the beginning of this chapter.
The choice is always yours.

ANALYZING YOUR AUDIENCE

Without the audience, there is no speech, and there is no speaker. The
audience is the reason for the speech. Too often, the beginning speaker
isn't even conscious of this fundamental truth. She spends an inordinate
amount of time and energy worrying about how she will be perceived
by the audience, without even once stopping to consider exactly who it
is she will be talking to. *Audience analysis* is the process that examines
the interests, knowledge, attitudes, and demographics of the audience.

The analysis of your audience is essential to your entire speech process. Without it, your chances of selecting, researching, and presenting
an interesting and captivating speech are severely limited. The process
of audience analysis should influence each of the previous four steps in
the topic and main-point selection process.

Therefore, the analysis should begin immediately as you select your
speech topic and main points. There are four areas of audience analysis
that you should examine as you select your topic and main points. They
are audience interest, knowledge, attitude, and demographics.

Audience Interest

Will the audience be interested in this topic? Hopefully, you as the
speaker will be interested in the topic you are considering. But will your
audience be interested? It was once stated that "there are no uninteresting topics, only uninterested listeners." The topic of flower arrange-
ments might be an extremely boring topic to a group of Hell's Angels,
but of pressing interest to a convention of florists. On the other hand,
the topic of motorcycle engine overhauling techniques would most
likely have all members of the motorcycle club hanging on the edge of
their motorcycle seats, while the florists would have walked out of the
auditorium long ago.

It's vital that you consciously shift your attention to your audience
and their interests, and not stay stuck on what is of interest only to you.
One definition of a bore is someone who talks about things that interest
only him. So begin thinking in terms of the other person—the listener
in your audience. This emphasis on being sensitive to what others are
interested in is helpful in your interpersonal life as well.

Audience Knowledge

The second area that you need to examine as you analyze your audience is their knowledge of the topic. After you've concluded your audience will be interested in the specific topic you would like to speak on, you have to determine the audience's knowledge of that topic.

You don't want to speak below their knowledge level of the topic. That could bore and perhaps even insult your audience. If you spoke on the topic of "Basic bodybuilding equipment" to a group of experienced bodybuilders, you might not only bore them, but you run the risk of insulting them too. On the other hand, you don't want to speak above the knowledge level of your audience either. To speak on the topic of "The joys of advanced calculus" to a group of students enrolled in beginning algebra may only confuse and frustrate them, because they have no knowledge of and experience in calculus.

Audience Attitude

Analyzing the attitude of the audience is the third area of examination. What is the attitude of the audience regarding your topic? Are they in favor? Are they opposed? Or are they neutral in attitude? If they are neutral, how might you present your material to arouse their interest? Or if they are hostile to your topic, how might you neutralize or lessen their hostility? You may even decide to eliminate the topic altogether if their attitude toward your topic is hostile.

Audience Demographics

The final area of analysis is audience demographics. Will the audience be male, female, or a mixture of both? What is the average age of the audience? What is the age range? What are the occupational backgrounds of the audience members? What are their educational backgrounds? Is their income high, low, or average? Are the members affiliated with a particular political, professional, or interest group?

One of the most important demographic factors you need to consider is the cultural backgrounds of your audience. No longer are the audiences of the United States strictly European American, but a mixture of many cultural heritages. African American, Asian American, Hispanic, Native American, and numerous other cultural backgrounds populate the audiences you will be addressing now and in the years to come.

To adopt and develop a spirit of cultural awareness and sensitivity is necessary and desirable if you are to be an effective speaker. It is not the intent of this book to describe the cultural differences of these various groups, but rather, to invite you to begin or continue exposing yourself to cultures different from your own.

Here are four ways you can begin your intercultural journey. First, you can interact with students in class who are culturally different from you. Initiate interaction during class activities and in group assignments. You can even invite them for lunch or dessert after class. Making friends is a wonderful way to learn about different cultures. Second, you can enroll in an intercultural communication course next semester. Such a class will provide you with a basic understanding of and appreciation for communication between cultures. You can also take any course that offers a cultural emphasis, such as Asian-American literature, African-American history, or Native-American art. Third, you might even attend special speaking functions or social gatherings hosted by one of the many cultural clubs on campus. And finally, you can read both fiction and non-fiction books that describe or reflect a particular cultural heritage.

By exposing yourself to the literature, experiences, and personalities of people from different cultures, you will increase your awareness and sensitivity to their way of seeing the world and themselves. Hopefully, this increased awareness and sensitivity will be reflected in the speech topics you select and the manner in which you develop them.

SPEECH PREPARATION QUESTIONNAIRE

Before you research your speech, you need to research your audience and the speaking occasion to ensure the success of your speech. The first step is to locate a contact person, someone who is in charge of the speaking event, and interview that individual over the phone or in person. It would also be wise to visit the auditorium or room where you will be speaking, if that's possible, to get a feel for the place. The questionnaire on the following page provides some questions you might want to ask the contact person.

COMMUNICATION ACTIVITIES

Personal Activities

1. **Brainstorming about ourselves**

   Make a list of the positive things about yourself following the brainstorming rules, and give yourself 10 minutes for the activity. Remember not to evaluate—quantity is the goal. How did it feel to brainstorm all these wonderful things about yourself? A little different and strange? We need to do things like this more often. It's good for our self-image.

Speech Preparation Questionnaire

Speaking Date_____ Time _____

Contact Person_____ Phone _____
Address_____

Speech Occasion _____
Topic requested _____
Speaking purpose: ____entertain ____inform ____persuade
Speech time limit_____

Facility Location_____
Directions _____
_____
Size of auditorium/room _____
Podium_____ Microphone_____ Lighting_____

Audience
Name of group _____
Age of group members_____
Cultural/ethnic considerations _____
_____
Interest in topic _____
_____
Knowledge of topic_____
_____
Opinion of topic _____
_____
Special considerations _____
_____

2. **Interviewing for intercultural speech topics**

   Conduct an informal 10-minute interview with a student in class or an individual at work who is of a different cultural background from yours. Ask him or her to brainstorm a list of topics that make them mad, glad, or sad. Once the individual has completed the list, invite them to explain any of the items in terms of cultural relevance or interest. Don't judge or evaluate their comments. Simply listen and learn.

3. **Do something silly**

   In keeping with our brainstorming rules, do something silly today. There must be a hundred things you used to do as a kid that you really enjoyed or got a kick out of. Think back.... What was it? When you remember what it was, go out and do it. Even if it's silly. We need to be kids again, and many of the things we enjoyed when we were younger will soothe our souls now that we're a little older.

Class Activities

1. **Increasing your cultural awareness through reading**

   Select one magazine, periodical, or newspaper that represents a specific cultural group. Your college library will have a number of such publications. Thumb through one magazine or newspaper and read two articles of interest. What is the perspective or point of view of the articles? Is it different from yours? How is the perspective similar? How did you feel about the articles? Be prepared to share your responses to this assignment in class.

2. **Group discussion: Brainstorming speech topics**

   Divide the class into groups of five or six students. Have each group brainstorm possible speech topics of interest for 10 minutes. All group members are to record the suggestions, so everyone will have a list of possible topics. Remember the rules of brainstorming—no evaluation, quantity not quality, the wilder the better, and combine ideas. Have fun with this activity. Be creative in your thinking!

3. **Group discussion: Audience analysis**

   Divide the class into groups of five or six students. The task is to brainstorm five reasons why an audience would purchase a new vacuum cleaner from the group. Each group is to brainstorm five different reasons for each of the following four audiences—a fraternity, a group of elementary school teachers, a motorcycle club, and a retirement home. Be prepared to discuss your lists with the class.

5

GATHERING YOUR MATERIAL
What You Sow Is What You Reap

The icy wind blasted against the thin walls of the tent as mammoth sheets of snow fell from the black sky above. Huddled in their warm tent, three Sherpa guides calmly sipped their tea in silence as they listened to the monstrous groans of nature outside. In their silence, they contemplated the ascent from the base camp to the first rim of Mt. Everest the next morning. During the hours that followed, not one word would be exchanged among the three men. Each would sit comfortably in the silence. At ease with one another and within themselves, they had nothing to say, and only the sounds of the storm filled the tent as they sat.

The three Americans in the tent beside theirs were busily discussing the departure from the base camp. They talked about the weather conditions, hoping the storm would subside by early morning. They reminisced about past expeditions. They noisily exaggerated their earlier achievement, as they argued over which of them was the most skilled climber. The tent was filled with the heated words of their good-natured arguments as the storm raged outside.

When asked many weeks after the expedition why he didn't always feel the need to talk, one of the Sherpa guides replied, "There is no need to talk, if there is nothing to say. I am comfortable with my silence." The American who posed the question couldn't really grasp the import of the Sherpa's answer.

Many years ago Dionysius warned, "Let your speech be better than silence, or be silent." Much of our American public speaking, in the classroom as well as in the public forum, often resembles the mindless chatter of our televisions. Superficial topics and unimportant issues characterize a great deal of what we bring to our podiums. This tabloid mentality of the mass media permeates our daily conversation.

We need to occasionally be silent in this noisy culture of ours. We need to quit talking and listen—really listen to others without constantly interrupting. We need to listen with our whole being, and not just with our ears. We need to turn off the television. We need to turn off the car stereo and simply hear the hum of the car engine as we drive. We need to turn off the Sony Walkman and listen to the rustling of the leaves and the wind in the trees.

We need to experience silence and see what it has to teach us about others and ourselves. All of nature and life is singing to us outside our tents, and we need to take the time to simply listen. Maybe then our speech will reflect a deeper understanding of life and all it has to offer.

Giving a speech involves much more than confidence, delivery practice, and direct eye contact. It requires that what we share with our audience is indeed important, interesting, and, ultimately, life enhancing. This chapter will help you in this area of speaking. We will examine the process of gathering the content material for your speech—what to look for, where to look, and how to record the information.

WHAT TO LOOK FOR

As you begin researching your speech topic, you must know what types of supporting material to look for. Although there are a variety of systems that classify supporting material, most speech experts will agree on the following seven: definitions, examples, explanations, comparisons, statistics, expert testimony, and visual aids.

Definitions

One of the most helpful and readily accessible forms of supporting material is the simple *definition*. The novice speaker often overlooks the dictionary on her desk as she begins the process of gathering material for her presentation. Yet a definition is not only a powerful tool in clarifying terms for the audience's understanding, it also helps to focus the speaker in her research and preparation of the speech itself. A practical use of a definition might be seen in a husband's attempt to convince his wife they should take a one-week vacation to Hawaii: "You know, Janet, *Webster's Dictionary* says a vacation should be 'a period of suspension of regular work or study.' I would define a vacation as eight days and seven nights in Hawaii. How would you like to vacate for awhile?"

You should always define the most important term or two for any speech. For example, if you were to give a talk on "Honesty in relationships," you would want to define the term *honesty,* and include that definition in the introduction or the first main point of the speech. You could simply say, "And what do I mean by *honesty*? Well, *Webster's Dictionary* defines *honesty* as 'the quality or fact of being truthful, sincere, or frank.'" It's always worthwhile to define your terms early in the speech to clarify and limit the scope of your presentation.

One thing you might keep in mind is that a definition should not confuse the audience. Try to avoid technical terms that need defining themselves or definitions that are too lengthy. Select definitions that are easily understood and brief. You don't want to lose your audience before you even get started.

Examples

We use examples every day to support our assertions and positions. If we tell a friend he's usually late for luncheon dates, one of the first things he'll most likely say is, "Oh, yeah, when have I ever been late?" In other words, he's asking us to give an example to support our assertion.

One of the most widely used supporting devices is the example. The *example* is a specific instance of a generalization or assertion. *The Random House Dictionary* (we're using a definition already) defines *example* as "One of a number of things, or a part of something, taken to show the character of the whole." Remember the husband attempting to convince his wife to visit Hawaii a few paragraphs ago? Well, he could use an example such as: "Honey, you're going to love Hawaii. It's such a beautiful place to relax. I was there once when I graduated from high school, and I was impressed with the lushness of the vegetation and the warmth and clarity of the water. I was never more relaxed in all my life."

A good rule of thumb is to have at least one example in each of your main points in the speech. The example is a powerful tool the speaker can use to paint a specific picture in the minds of the audience.

Examples can be brief or detailed, factual or hypothetical. If an example is factual and familiar to your audience, you need only refer to it briefly, as your audience is acquainted with the incident. If you're speaking about famous sports achievements, you could briefly refer to the example of Mark McGwire breaking Roger Maris's home run record. If the audience is not familiar with an example you are using, you will need to develop it in more detail, with names, dates, and facts. A more detailed example is often called an *illustration*. These illustrations can take the form of anecdotes, personal experiences, stories, or parables.

A *factual example* is an instance or incident that actually took place. Suppose you are speaking about the advantages of buying flood insurance. Your example could be drawn from a family who had their damaged home replaced after the 1998 El Niño rains, and the bill was paid by the insurance company.

A *hypothetical example,* on the other hand, can also be impressive. You might put the audience in the shoes of an imaginary homeowner who had a home destroyed by a flood and was not covered by flood insurance: "Suppose you own a home and choose not to purchase flood insurance. Your home is destroyed by a flood. How do you pay for the thousands of dollars in damage? How will you cope with the stress of the added financial burden?" A hypothetical example is also called a *hypothetical situation.* It can be extremely effective in getting your audience to consider a situation from a different point of view.

Explanations

An *explanation* is used to make an idea clear and easily seen in the mind's eye of the audience. Once again, the husband could use an explanation when convincing his wife to visit Hawaii: "I'm convinced you'll love Hawaii because you enjoy beautiful scenery, you like to swim in warm water, and whether you admit it or not, you do like to get away from the kids." How could she turn this down? But she's still holding firm to her refusal to go to Hawaii.

Well, let's leave those two for a while and examine the three types of explanations you can use: analysis, exposition, and description.

Analysis is the process of explaining or studying something by examining its parts. You might want to explain to your audience how to bake a cake by breaking the process into three parts: gathering the materials, mixing the materials, and, finally, baking the cake.

The purpose of *exposition* is to give your audience information that will increase their knowledge of a topic. Much of any speech is devoted to expounding or explaining so the audience understands more about the topic. A speech on how to make money selling real estate, grow a garden, or improve communication within a marriage will use exposition.

Description uses the five senses of taste, touch, sight, smell, and hearing to let the audience know what is being presented. Often the use of description is the most powerful method of painting a picture in the minds of your audience. Suppose you are trying to describe a beach scene to your audience. Instead of simply saying "It was a beautiful beach," you might describe the scene by saying, "Imagine yourself sitting in the warm sand (touch), and the sound of the waves lapping on the shore (hearing) relaxes you. You smell the salt air (smell), and the blue ocean stretches out as far as you can see (sight)." Which one describes the scene in more detail? The use of description can have a powerful impact on the minds of your audience.

Comparisons

A *comparison* presents qualities or features that are similar. One of the most effective ways to present a new idea is to compare it to something that is familiar to the audience. Often comparisons attempt to show the connection between what the audience knows and what they do not know. The husband in our continuing vacation saga could use a comparison such as: "Hawaii's water is like Florida's, only clearer. The climate of Hawaii is like Southern California's. And the people of Hawaii are as friendly as our own family."

A comparison can be either figurative or literal. *Figurative comparisons* describe similarities between things that are otherwise different. "He's as slow as molasses" or "The heart is like a pump" are examples of figurative comparisons.

A *literal comparison* is an actual comparison. This type of comparison gives your listeners a clear mental picture of what you're talking about. You can tell your audience that the airplane weighed as much as seven pickup trucks or the tomato was the size of a softball.

Noting differences between two entities is using *contrast*. Here the emphasis is on differences rather than similarities. An example of contrast can be seen when a mother tells her daughter that when she was 20 years old, college cost $3,000 in annual tuition. But now, an annual tuition bill of $30,000 is not unusual. Things sure have changed.

Statistics

Many of your listeners will be interested in and impressed by statistics. *Statistics* are numerical facts, such as: one out of four Americans will experience some form of cancer in his or her lifetime; 50 percent of all marriages will end in divorce; and Z-Company stock doubled in the past five years. Once again, in his attempts to persuade his wife to go to Hawaii, the husband might use a statistic: "One out of every three Americans prefers vacationing in Hawaii to any other place in the world."

Wisely used, statistics can have a powerful impact on your audience. Unwisely used, they can bore, confuse, and even deceive the audience. When using statistics, try to keep them simple and easily understood by the average audience member.

There are some important rules to keep in mind when you use statistical information in your speech.

1. Your most important concern is the accuracy of the statistics you are using. You should take statistics from reliable sources. Is the magazine, book, journal, newspaper, or Web site a trusted, proven source?

Is the author or the researcher of the statistics a credible source? Check these things out before using the information.

2. Your statistics should be recent. What may have been true just five or ten years ago could be outdated now. Try to have your statistics reflect research that is no more than five years old. The more recent, the better.

3. Limit your use of statistics. Once you have researched a topic thoroughly and have collected reams of statistical information about your subject, there is a tendency to want to use all of the data in your speech. If you did, you would run the serious risk of overwhelming your audience. You must realize that your listeners can accept and remember only a few statistics during the course of a speech. It is better to have a few well-placed statistics in your speech than to overload your listeners with an avalanche of numbers. Choose those statistics wisely.

4. Use your statistics for comparative purposes. For instance, when discussing the number of lawyers in America, you might tell your audience that in 1997, one out of every 320 Americans was a lawyer. But the picture changes when you compare that statistic to 1967, when only one out of every 1,210 Americans was a lawyer. The comparison gets even more interesting if you compare our statistics with those of Japan, where in 1997 only one out of every 8,270 Japanese citizens was a lawyer.

5. Round off your statistics. Present your statistics in a way that will make them easy for your audience to understand. Instead of saying the average annual wage of a field-worker in Chile is $388.73, round off your statistic so that it will be more easily heard and remembered by the audience. With this in mind, the average wage of the field-worker in Chile becomes $390 annually. Much easier to hear and remember.

6. Use visual aids to present your statistics. For many people, it is difficult to visualize even the simplest statistic as it is being rattled off by the speaker. If the speaker shoots out too many statistics and numbers, the audience often will simply tune the speaker out. The human organism avoids pain and suffering, in the auditorium as well as in personal life. If you have a lot of statistics to present, you might try presenting them in the form of a visual aid—a chart, graph, table, or diagram. We examine this in more detail later in the chapter.

Expert Testimony

The testimony of an expert or authority on a particular subject adds credibility to your speech. The most important benefit of *expert testimony* is to show your audience that you are not alone in your thinking—your ideas and convictions are also held by experts in the field.

You're probably wondering if that wife has decided to visit Hawaii yet. She hasn't. What will it take to convince her? Maybe the husband could present some expert testimony: "Sylvia Bass, our travel agent, told me that of all the places she's vacationed in the world, Hawaii is her favorite." The wife is smiling, but still shaking her head. Well, while she's deciding, let's discuss who to interview if you plan to offer expert testimony in your speech.

You must turn to experts or authorities when researching your speech topics. If your subject is drug abuse, your attention turns to the medical doctor and the drug abuse therapist. If your subject is inflation, your attention turns to the economist. If your subject is engine repair, your attention turns to the auto mechanic. The source of expert testimony changes with each topic.

There are two ways you can support your views with the expert testimony of others. You can quote them word for word, or you can paraphrase what they said in your own words. You can paraphrase the expert's testimony if the material is longer than a couple of sentences in length or to simplify the statement in an accurate manner. The shorter the quotation, the greater the impact it will have on your audience.

Because the information you are presenting is not yours, you must *give credit* where credit is due. You must orally document the testimony by telling the audience who said it, where you got the information, and the date of the testimony. It may be stated as simply as, "In the June 1998 issue of *The California Therapist,* Dr. Salvador Minuchin states...," or "President Clinton, in the June 13, 1998, issue of *Time* magazine, warns..."

You can add more credibility to your expert, especially if your authority is not well known to the audience, by presenting some background information before you give his or her testimony. For example, with the first quotation from Dr. Minuchin, you could preface his remarks by adding, "Dr. Minuchin is a world-famous family therapist, the author of three textbooks on family therapy, and an internationally acclaimed lecturer on family dysfunction." Keep in mind that your documentation and background information on your expert have more impact if you present them *before* you give the testimony.

Visual Aids

The old Chinese saying "One picture is worth a thousand words" holds true in public speaking as well. The final category of supporting material is *visual aids*. Visual aids can improve your speech by focusing the attention of your listeners, making your ideas easier to understand, and helping your listeners remember what you said.

This is our husband's final attempt to convince his wife to vacation in Hawaii. He will use a series of visual aids: "Honey, just look at these recent snapshots Sylvia took on her last vacation to Hawaii. Look at the beautiful water. Doesn't the sand look clean? Can you imagine yourself on that beach right now?" She finally says "Yes!" The visual aids did the trick! She's going to Hawaii. But we're not, so we need to examine different visual-aid forms.

The various forms of visual aids include the speaker himself, the chalkboard, objects, models, drawings and sketches, charts, and electronic media. Let's examine each of these forms of visual aids in more detail.

The *speaker himself* can be a very powerful visual aid. Not only do dress and appearance help provide the audience with a strong visual message and a means of evaluating the overall message of the speaker, but body movement, gestures, and facial expressions can also play an important role in helping the audience visualize the speech.

The speaker's body can demonstrate how to move when skiing, dancing, and kicking. Her hands and gestures can show how to massage a neck, hold chopsticks, or throw a football. Her face can display a range of emotions that can help the audience visualize a scene from a story or anecdote. Don't be afraid to act out or demonstrate portions of your speech that can be appreciated and understood only when they are seen by the audience.

The *chalkboard* is another readily accessible visual aid that may help the audience visualize portions of your speech. Chalkboard use is best for impromptu speeches, when the speaker has no preparation time to construct a prepared drawing or chart. The disadvantages of chalkboard use are many. Often the speaker will speak to the chalkboard and not the audience. And the speaker's body will partly obscure much of what is being put up on the board. The chalkboard should be used only as a last resort. If you prepare properly for your speech, you will have adequate time to construct a prepared drawing or chart that will prove much more valuable to the audience.

The *object itself* is an excellent visual aid. Showing the audience the actual computer, quilt, vase, or surfboard leaves little to misinterpretation. Often, however, the actual object is impractical to bring to the classroom or auditorium.

A *model* makes a very helpful visual aid. A model is a representation that serves as a manageable copy of the object itself. If you were giving a speech on airplanes, A-frame cabins, or the water molecule, a model would serve as an effective visual aid. One thing to remember about models is they don't have to be works of art. One speaker spent more than $40 having a plastic model of a jet engine constructed, when a balloon would have done just fine. Make sure that your model is large enough for your audience to see, and that it gives your audience a rough idea of what you're talking about.

Drawings and sketches are perhaps the easiest of all visual aids to construct. Now, you might be thinking, "I'm no artist," and skip the rest of this paragraph. But hold on for a moment. As in model construction, your drawing or sketch doesn't have to be a work of art. With a few felt pens, a compass, a straightedge, and some patience, you can create a drawing or sketch that will add clarity and dimension to the speech.

Keep your drawings simple. Don't overload the audience with unnecessary details when a stick figure sketch would suffice. Make your drawings, sketches, and lettering large enough so that the people in the back row will be able to see them. After you're done with the first draft of the drawing, move as far away from the drawing as the back row of your audience and give it a glance. If the drawing can be seen from there, fine. If not, it's back to the drawing board for a larger version.

The colors used in your drawing or sketch should stand out at a distance. Colors such as black and red on white cardboard are easily seen. Pink and yellow on a white background cannot be seen. Use 2 × 3-foot white cardboard (the kind you buy at stationery stores for a couple of dollars) for drawing your sketches; they stand up better on easels than sheets of regular paper do.

Charts permit the speaker to present a wealth of information in very little space. Word charts, number charts, steps in a process, organizational flowcharts, and maps add important visual dimensions to any speech. Line graphs, pie graphs, and bar graphs can also be utilized to present statistics so that large amounts of data can be seen at one glance.

When constructing a chart, keep it as simple as possible. The lettering and numbering should be large enough to be seen by all your audience. Using lettering and numbering so small that only the speaker can see them is a common mistake made by those speakers who forget the chart is for the audience to see, not for the speaker.

Microsoft's PowerPoint, Adobe Persuasion, and *Lotus Freelance Graphics* are three excellent software programs that can be helpful in designing and constructing much more elaborate visual aids and multimedia presentations into your speeches. These relatively simple to use computer-assisted graphics programs allow you to design and combine highly professional looking charts, graphs, slides, photographs, and video clips into your speeches. You might consider enrolling in a computer applications class or workshop that teaches you how to use one of these programs.

Finally, the use of *electronic media,* such as videotape playback recorders, overhead projectors, and slide projectors can also be considered when planning the visual-aid portion of your talk. When you consider their use, remember that electronic media may not be appropriate for some speeches. If you have only five minutes to get a group of people to vote in tomorrow's election, electronic media may not be the best approach to convince your audience, because five minutes does not give you adequate time for preparation. On the other hand, if you're trying to convince a group of teenagers to not drink and drive, and you are given adequate preparation time, a videotape of a fatal car accident scene may have an impact on your audience that words cannot provide.

After considering the advantages and disadvantages of using electronic media, it would be wise for you to practice with the device ahead of time. When you practice your speech, include the use of the machine. There's nothing more embarrassing than trying in front of an audience to figure out how some machine works.

Suggestions for Using Visual Aids

If you decide to use any visual aids in your speech, here are some recommendations you may find helpful:

1. Make sure the visual aid is large enough to be seen.
2. Keep your visual aids simple. Your audience must be able to grasp their meaning immediately.
3. Use visual aids only if they clarify or reinforce a point you are trying to make. Don't overdo the use of visual aids. You don't want to overwhelm or overload the audience.
4. Show your visual aids only when you are talking about them. When you are not using a visual aid, place it out of sight. You don't want to distract your listeners.
5. Never pass your visual aids around to the audience. You will lose their attention. No matter how mature or sophisticated your audience appears, they're all kids at heart, and you'll lose their attention as they fiddle, tug, stretch, and bang your visual aid.
6. Maintain eye contact with your audience when using your visual aid.
7. Don't talk to your visual aid. Talk to your audience.
8. Practice with your visual aid. A common mistake for the novice speaker is to think that she will know how to handle a visual aid without ever practicing with it. Get the feel of your visual aids before you give your speech.

WHERE TO LOOK FOR SPEECH INFORMATION

Now that you have an idea of what to look for when you're researching your speech, we need to spend some time discussing where to look for this information. There are three primary areas to explore—your own experience and knowledge, library resources, and interviewing.

Your Own Experience and Knowledge

Most people rush off to the library when they are faced with the prospect of researching a speech topic. And by doing so, they overlook one of the richest sources of speech information—their own experience and knowledge.

If you sit quietly for a moment or two and scan your prior experience and knowledge of the speech topic you've selected, scenes from the past, bits and pieces of knowledge from old lectures or conversations, and anecdotes from personal experience will parade past your mind's eye. Each one potentially provides unique and interesting information for the content of your speech. A woman giving a speech on parenting may remember stories about her parents, movies that depicted the struggles and rewards of parenting, the highlights of an old college lecture on raising children, and an anecdote or two about raising her own children. This information from past knowledge and experience serves as an original and colorful source of speech information.

The brainstorming technique can be utilized here when surveying your past experience and knowledge. Simply jotting down every related experience and piece of knowledge, no matter how small or trivial, will provide a springboard from which you can begin your research.

Library Resources

The library might not be your first choice for exciting places to visit on a Friday evening, but it does serve as one of the most rewarding sources of speech information. Every library, regardless of size, usually provides the following sources of information that you will need to research your speech:

The *computer* or *card catalog* indexes all of the library's information by author, title, and subject. This catalog is your primary guide to the books in the library. If you are unfamiliar with its operation, ask the librarian on duty for assistance. He will be more than happy to assist you.

Magazines and *periodicals* are another source of information for your speech. The *Reader's Guide to Periodical Literature* will be your most valuable resource for locating magazine and periodical articles that are related to your speech topic. The advantage of magazine or periodical information is that it is generally more current than information provided by books and encyclopedias. The *Reader's Guide* indexes the articles of more than 130 U.S. journals on a wide range of topics. In addition, you may wish to consult other indexes such as the *Education Index* for topics related to education or the *Index to Behavioral Sciences and Humanities.*

Quotation books provide another rich source of information for your speech. *Bartlett's Familiar Quotations,* a reference book containing more than 1,500 pages of quotations on every topic imaginable, is one of the most popular collections of quotations. One-third of the book is an index to help you find a suitable quotation on just about any topic. Your library should have a copy of *Familiar Quotations,* along with a few other similar reference works. A quotation often provides an ideal beginning or ending to your speech.

Your library should have one or two of your local daily *newspaper indexes,* in addition to the *New York Times Index.* Although newspapers don't always provide the most scholarly writing on a given topic, the articles can be a source of recent and local information for your speech.

The final library resource we will mention is a research tool you may already have access to in your home or office, and that's the Internet. The *Internet* is a worldwide collection of interconnected computer networks. If you don't already know how to access information from the Internet, you might want to enroll in an introductory Internet class or workshop. In a few hours, you can learn to surf the Net and discover additional information for your speeches. For the purposes of this book, however, we will only discuss subject searches and how to evaluate the soundness of the information accessed.

You can research your speech topic by using subject-based search engines such as Yahoo!, AltaVista, Infoseek, and Excite NetSearch. Once you access the search engine's home page, you will get a list of links to a number of general topic areas including News, Science, Education, Business, Sports, Sociology, Government, and Society. After you click on one of these topic areas, you will get a list of subtopics. When you click on one of the subtopics, you will get a screen that further divides the topic into smaller and more specific subtopics until you find the Web site you want to research for your speech topic.

Unlike the printed material in a library, which has been evaluated and approved of by the library staff, the majority of information on the Internet has not been subjected to editorial review by an acquisitions staff. Instead, much of the information on the Internet exists only in electronic form. Just about anybody with a computer and a link can post their writings on the Internet. So you need to be careful when selecting information for inclusion in your speech.

Here are three criteria you can use when selecting information. First, is the author of the Web article or document clearly identified? Is he or she an expert in the field? Are his or her credentials and qualifications provided? Second, many documents on the Internet are published by organizations, rather than specific authors, so you must evaluate the credibility of the particular business, agency, or interest group whose article you are considering. And finally, you must consider the recency of the document you are evaluating. A good rule of thumb is to consider only those articles that have been published in the past three years. If any Web article fails one of these criteria, don't use it in your speech. There are too many other more credible and reliable documents to choose from.

Interviewing

The final source of speech information we will discuss is the *interviewing* of experts. Although many speakers are reluctant to ask for an interview from a local expert, the rewards of doing so can go beyond those of simply giving a well-researched speech. Many a friendship, both professional and personal, and many a job have blossomed because of a 15-minute interview.

For a given speech, don't interview more than one or two experts, because the interview process involves more time and effort than you might imagine.

The first step in conducting an interview is to decide *whom* you want to talk with. If your speech is on sleeping pills, you may want to speak with a pharmacist or a physician. If your topic is automobile engine repair, you may want to talk with an auto mechanic who specializes in engine overhauling. Or if your speech is on the planet Jupiter, you may want to interview an astronomy instructor at a local college or university.

The second step is to *request an interview.* Whether you request an interview in person, over the telephone, or in a formal letter, keep your request brief and friendly. Let the person know who you are, that you are researching a speech topic in his or her field of expertise, and that you would like a 15-minute interview at his or her convenience (not yours). If the person cannot or will not grant an interview, thank him or her for the time and try the next candidate. If he or she agrees to the interview, great!

The third step is to write a list of *questions* for the interview itself. This should be done only *after* you have researched the topic from your own knowledge and experience and have conducted your library search for material. This prior research will enable you to ask more enlightened, specific, and articulate questions.

The fourth step is the *interview itself.* Be punctual. Nothing is more annoying to your interviewee than for you to arrive late to a meeting that you requested. Dress up for the interview. Don't arrive in your tank top and old Levi's. Show a little respect. And stick to your time limit of 15 minutes. You can cover a lot of territory in that period of time, as long as you stick to the task at hand. Bring your list of questions and a pen to jot down noteworthy remarks. At the end, thank the interviewee.

Finally, after you've returned from the interview, take a moment out to write a brief *thank-you card* or letter to the person you interviewed. The few minutes and the cost of the stamp will add that touch of class that few interviewers ever consider.

HOW TO RECORD YOUR SPEECH INFORMATION

Now that you have a better idea of what to look for and where to look for it, let's briefly discuss how to record the information you will be using.

In your research, you will find a variety of examples, quotations, statistics, and comparisons that you will want to collect. You may not use all of the information, and you may not even know the order in which you will present it. So, you will have to find some way of recording all this data. People have used everything from professional calligraphy paper to the clean side of a McDonald's hamburger wrapper to record their speech information.

The best material to use for recording your information is the 4 × 6-inch index card. You can purchase a pack of 50 cards at any drug or stationery store for a couple dollars. Index cards are recommended because sorting and rearranging your material is much easier when each piece of information is recorded on a separate index card, as opposed to one large sheet of paper.

When recording your research material, you should note the author's name and book title, magazine, newspaper, or Web site address on the upper left-hand side of the card. If your evidence was taken during an interview, list the interviewee's name and professional background. The quotation, statistic, example, and so on should be recorded in the middle of the card. A finished note card should look something like this:

Randy Fujishin

Gifts from the Heart, Acada Books, 1998

"No loving relationship can be sustained
without giving the gifts of communication."

When researching your material, you should collect about *three times* the amount of material you will need for the speech. In the average five-minute speech, you will most likely need about two minutes of research information. So if you read all your researched information orally, and it takes you about six minutes, you probably have enough information to choose from for the speech.

Regarding the number of sources you should consult, you should present at least three different sources of information. Three is the minimum. Fewer than that would not ensure sufficient depth or breadth of research.

A final word of caution would be to begin your research as soon as possible. Most people tend to procrastinate and let things slide to the last minute. But tardiness in your research will only increase your anxiety and wreak havoc on your sleep. Don't wait until the night before you are scheduled to speak to begin your research. That will only make you old before your time.

COMMUNICATION ACTIVITIES

Personal Activities

1. **What happened on the day you were born?**

   Have you ever wondered what was going on the day you made your entry into the world? Here's a fun research project. Go to the library and look up a *New York Times* newspaper published on the date (month, day, and year) you were born. You'll probably have to go into the back of the library and use the microfilm machine, but be of good cheer. It'll be well worth your efforts. Who says research is boring?

2. **Whom do you trust?**

   Make a list of three magazines, newspapers, or other publications you trust in terms of the reliability of their information and reporting. Would you have listed these three publications 10 years ago? How about 10 years from now? What publications would you not accept as being reliable or truthful?

3. **Whom would you have dinner with?**

   If you could interview (over dinner) anyone (either living or dead) for three hours, who would he or she be? That's any human being who has ever lived or is now living! Why did you select this individual? Would you have interviewed him or her 10 years ago, if you were given this fantasy choice? How about 10 years from now? What do you think you would learn during the interview?

Class Activities

1. **Your dream home speech**

   Take a moment and pretend you have just inherited $5 million! You can live anywhere in the world. Where would you choose to live? Pick a specific location (the city of Hilo, Hawaii, as opposed to "somewhere in the Pacific"). Once you've decided on a specific place, go to the library and see if you can locate three sources of information on your dream home location. After reading about this place, does it still hold its appeal? What did you learn about this place? What did you learn about yourself? Prepare, practice, and present a three- to five-minute speech discussing three interesting facts or facets about this dream location. Your speech should include an introduction, body, and conclusion.

2. **Overcoming my fear speech**

   There's a good chance at this very moment, in the back of your mind somewhere, you're fearful or worried about something. It might be a small lump on your neck, the possibility of a relationship breakup, or anxiety over being late on an installment payment. No matter what your fear or worry is, make a research project out of it. Think of one or two people you could talk to or interview who are experts, or at least experienced, in this area of concern of yours. Whom did you interview? What did you learn about your fear? What actions can you take to eliminate, decrease, or accept this fear? Prepare, practice, and present a three- to five-minute speech about three insights you discovered about this fear. Your speech should include an introduction, body, and conclusion.

3. **Intercultural speech**

   Select a culture, other than your own, that you would like to learn more about. Research at least three written sources, and interview one individual from the culture you selected. Prepare, practice, and deliver a three- to five-minute speech presenting three interesting facts you learned about this culture. Your speech should include an introduction, body, and conclusion.

6

ORGANIZING YOUR SPEECH
Keeping It Simple

Have you ever experienced a time in your life when everything seemed to hit all at once? A hundred things to do. Appointments to keep. Projects to complete. Unfinished business pressing in from all sides.

Sam's first year of college teaching was like that. He was 23 years old, teaching three classes as a part-time instructor at a local community college, attending graduate school, volunteering a couple hours a day as a teacher's aide at a local day-care center, and washing dishes at the Garrett Restaurant in the evenings. In addition, Sam was conducting communication workshops for college students every other Sunday at a local church.

Somehow, he managed to juggle all those responsibilities for the first three months of the year, until gradually he noticed changes in his behavior. He was getting angry over little things. And he wasn't sleeping as well as he once had. Getting up in the morning was becoming more difficult, and Sam found himself just lying in bed staring at the ceiling after the buzzer would sound.

Sam has since learned that these are some of the telltale symptoms of depression. But then, all he knew was that getting up in the morning was becoming more and more difficult. Knowing that something was wrong, Sam wanted to talk to someone about his situation. But he didn't have the money to see a therapist. He was too embarrassed to share his problem with his family, and too proud to discuss it with his friends. So he was stuck.

One Saturday morning, not long after, as Sam was sitting on the back porch of his second-story apartment, Annie shouted up to him with an invitation for coffee. Annie Loveless was a friendly, 76-year-old woman who lived by herself in the apartment directly under his. Annie was slender, gentle, and very wise. After her second husband died nine years earlier in Hollywood, she came up to northern California to live. The years had been good to her, and she seemed to glide through life with ease and grace.

After pouring a second cup of coffee, she asked Sam if he had been feeling well. He lied and said he was fine. A long silence followed his response, and Annie whispered, "I once heard that God invented time so everything wouldn't happen all at once." Sam smiled weakly and remained silent as he held his cup.

"You have a long life ahead of you," she continued. "Don't complicate and confuse your life with too many things, too many responsibilities. You need to ease your burden by cutting some things out. I think you need to simplify your life a little."

Annie was a good friend, and she had come to know Sam well during the year and a half he had lived at the apartment. Her words hit him with a force few have. During the next two weeks, Sam quit his dishwashing job at the restaurant, said good-bye to all those kids at the daycare center, and taught the college Sunday School class once a month instead of twice.

With only his teaching and graduate school to occupy his time, Sam felt the weight of the world had been lifted from his shoulders. His anger gradually subsided. His sleep began to return to normal. And soon, Sam discovered it was even easy to wake in the morning when the buzzer went off.

Not all responsibilities can be cast aside. Not all lives can be simple and uncomplicated in the web of relationships, ties, and duties accumulated over the years. But we do have freedom to make choices. We don't have to say yes to every request that is placed before us. Sometimes we need to choose simplicity over complexity. One or two good friends, instead of 10 or 15. One or two organizational memberships, instead of seven or eight. A desk empty of clutter, rather than one piled high with old papers, books, unanswered mail, and yesterday's lunch wrappings. One single painting adorning a wall, instead of five. There is beauty and freedom in simplicity.

Keep It Simple

A young pastor, intent on impressing the congregation with his theological education, developed a lengthy, complicated, and verbose sermon style. The congregation would stir restlessly, eyeing the clock on the wall, as this young pastor droned on and on in his sermons, bringing up point after point after point.

This continued for some time, until one Sunday morning, the pastor's wife, also frustrated with his long sermons, slipped him a note before he went up to speak. At the top of the note was written, "KISS." He smiled as he glanced over to his wife. Then he noticed at the bottom of the note, "Keep It Simple, Stupid."

Hopefully, you will never receive such a note. But the recommendation to "keep it simple" is one of the wisest bits of advice you will ever receive.

Your speech must be designed in a structure that is easy to follow if you are to accomplish your goal of having the audience listen to your words, remember your points, and act on your recommendations.

Far too many novice speakers talk in a style that is difficult to follow. The listener gets lost in a maze of unrelated thoughts and ideas, with no clear theme connecting the endless parade of words. We often lose interest, and perhaps become annoyed with a speaker who cannot present her thoughts in a readily understood fashion.

SPEECH ORGANIZATION

Now that you've decided on a speech topic and researched your subject, we will examine how you will organize all this material into a structure that is easy for your listeners to follow.

More than 2,000 years ago, the Greek philosopher Plato said that every speech should have only three parts: an introduction, a body, and a conclusion. Just like our existence: birth, life, and death. This simple formula for speech organization still holds true today. Whether you're giving a two-minute impromptu talk at a wedding reception or a 20-minute sales presentation to a group of prospective buyers, the organization of your speech is the same.

Let's preview the basic functions of the introduction, body, and conclusion before we launch into a more detailed examination of each of these three components.

The *introduction* should capture the attention of the audience, clearly state what your speech is about, and preview the main points of your talk. Your introduction should comprise only 10 to 15 percent of your total speaking time.

The *body* of the speech contains the two or three main points of your talk. Supporting material necessary to develop each point is contained in the body, along with clearly stated transitions between each point. The body of the speech should comprise 75 to 85 percent of your total speaking time.

And the *conclusion* of the speech presents a summary of your main points and a final thought or appeal to leave your audience with. The conclusion should be brief and should comprise only 5 to 10 percent of your total speaking time.

THE BODY

We'll examine the body of the speech before we discuss the introduction. This may seem a little odd, but we need to realize that we can't work on our attention getter and preview of main points in the introduction until we know what the main points will be and how they will be organized. Let's begin with the main-point selection and organization.

Main-Point Selection

The specific purpose, you will remember, states the speaking purpose and divides the speech into its key parts or main points. The remainder of the body of the speech develops, clarifies, explains, or proves those main points. Let's examine one specific purpose.

> *Specific Purpose:* To inform the audience about three uses of public speaking training.

As you see, the specific purpose establishes the goal in speaking (to inform the audience) and what you want to share (about three uses of public speaking training). What are those three uses? They constitute the three main points of the speech. In complete sentence form, those three points were:

> *Main Points:* I. Public speaking improves your presentational skills.
> II. Public speaking helps you become more effective in business.
> III. Public speaking improves your self-image.

Selecting main points is not difficult, as long as you remember that each of the implied areas of the specific purpose will be one of the main points of your speech.

Let's have you try your hand at providing three main points for a specific purpose statement. Suppose you had to share with your audience three things that make you happy. Any three things that bring you joy, make you feel good, give you a rush. The specific purpose statement would be:

> *Specific Purpose:* To share with the audience three things that make me happy.

Now, complete the main points with three things that make you happy. Use short, *complete sentences* for each point.

    I. _____

   II. _____

  III. _____

Now that wasn't too difficult, was it? You've just completed outlining your first main-point structure for the body of an informative speech. Not bad!

Main-Point Organizational Patterns

For your purposes as beginning speakers, the following five main-point orders will most likely suit your needs. Topical order, time order, spatial order, advantage-disadvantage order, and problem-solution order. Each of these five main-point organizational patterns is designed to present your main points in a way that is easy for the audience to understand and remember, and satisfies the requirements of your specific purpose.

Topical Order

In topical order, the order of the main points is up to the discretion of the speaker. The main points can go from specific to general, from least important to most important. Often the topic suggests its own arrangement of main points. Look at how the following example makes use of this organizational pattern.

> *Specific Purpose:* To describe three characteristics of a good marriage.
>   **I.** The partners share in open communication.
>   **II.** The partners support the personal growth of one another.
> **III.** The partners resolve conflict in a nonthreatening manner.

Now that you've gotten the hang of topical order, let's have you complete the following:

> *Specific Purpose:* To discuss the three things I appreciate about my college education.

    I. _____

   II. _____

  III. _____

Time Order

Time order is the kind of organizational pattern in which the main points follow a chronological order or sequence. It shows your audience there is a definite order in which the main points develop. The order of main points is not left to the discretion of the speaker; but rather, it is determined by the process itself. This type of organizational pattern works well with speeches that describe how something is made, how something happened, or how something works. Notice the time order in the following example:

Specific Purpose: To explain how to bake cookies.
    I. The first step is to gather your materials.
    II. The second step is to prepare the ingredients.
    III. The third step is to bake the cookies.

Now, try your hand at providing the main points for the following specific purpose, utilizing time order:

Specific Purpose: To explain how I wake up in the morning.

    I. _____

    II. _____

    III. _____

Spatial Order

The third organizational pattern we will examine in this chapter is spatial order. In spatial order, the main points are arranged in physical or geographical sequence. This pattern could be employed in a speech that described the floor plan of your house, the digestive tract of the human body, or the structure of a guitar. See if you can visualize the spatial structure in the following example:

Specific Purpose: To describe the arrangement of the Town Hall.
    I. The first floor contains the receptionist area and clerks' offices.
    II. The second floor houses the city officials' offices.
    III. The third floor stores the city records.

How would you list the main points for the following specific purpose statement?

Specific Purpose: To describe the three parts of a whole egg (not a scrambled egg).

    I. _____

II. _____

III. _____

Advantage-Disadvantage Order

The fourth main-point order is advantage-disadvantage. There might be a time when you want to present both sides of a case or proposal. The purpose of your speech would be to fairly and equally communicate the pros and cons of an issue or case. Here's an example of advantage-disadvantage main-point order.

> *Specific Purpose:* To inform the audience about the advantages and disadvantages of enrolling in a summer school class.
> I. There are advantages to enrolling in a summer school class.
>   A. A summer school class enables you to focus your attention on one subject.
>   B. A summer school class is completed in only four to six weeks.
> II. There are disadvantages to enrolling in a summer school class.
>   A. A summer school class requires longer daily class meetings.
>   B. A summer school class requires three times the daily homework.

See if you can think of the subpoints for this advantage-disadvantage speech.

> *Specific Purpose:* To inform the audience about the advantages and disadvantages of working full-time while attending college.
> I. There are advantages to working full-time while attending college.
>
>   A. _____
>   B. _____
> II. There are disadvantages to working full-time while attending college.
>
>   A. _____
>   B. _____

Problem-Solution Order

The fifth main-point order is problem-solution. Many times you will want to propose a specific solution to an existing problem. This is a persuasive speech structure that will be discussed in Chapter 9, but for now, we will briefly outline the format known as problem-solution order.

> *Proposition:* You should support a comprehensive federal health care program.
>   I. Currently, millions of Americans are denied adequate health care.
>   II. A comprehensive federal health care program would solve this problem.
> III. A comprehensive federal health care program would be the best solution to this problem.

See if you can construct three points to this problem-solution proposition.

> *Proposition:* You should support an 8 percent federal income tax.

    I. _____

   II. _____

  III. _____

Now that you've chosen your main points and the organizational pattern you will use, you need to turn your attention to selecting the developmental material. How your audience will receive, understand, and appreciate what you have to say will depend largely on how you develop the main points of the body.

In the previous chapter, you learned how to research a speech topic, using the 4 × 6-inch note card method—storing each piece of research evidence on a note card. Let's assume you've already completed your research of a speech topic, so you now have three times the amount of material required for your talk. Now we must begin the task of selecting the appropriate supporting material for your main points.

Selecting Your Developmental Material

The easiest method for selecting supporting material for your speech is called the "pile method." To use the "pile method," simply place the various 4 × 6-inch research cards in one of three piles (if you have three main points), according to content. At the end of this process, each pile or stack will contain various definitions, statistics, expert testimony, examples, stories, comparisons, explanations, or visual aids that support a particular main point.

Now the fun part begins—the selection of the actual pieces of supporting material you will use for each main point. Here are some suggestions that will guide you in your selection as you stare at the various piles of research cards scattered on your bed or desk:

Have at least one piece of evidence for each point. Provide at least one piece of evidence to support each of your main points. This will provide a solid base of support for your speech.

Provide a variety of supporting material. Don't just give statistics in each point or tell anecdotes throughout your speech. Provide a variety of supporting material for your listeners to consider. If you researched your topic sufficiently, you should have little difficulty giving your audience a variety of supporting material.

Distribute your supporting material evenly. Give each main point of your speech equal development. Don't invest three pieces of evidence on one main point, and not support the other two points. Provide the listener with an equal balance of supporting material for each point.

Adapt your material to the particular audience. This suggestion is vitally important if your message is to be received by your audience. In a previous chapter we discussed the components of audience analysis: audience interest, knowledge, attitude, and demographics. Remember that audiences respond favorably to information that relates to their interests, their knowledge, their attitudes, and their demographics. Adapt your research information in ways that your particular audience can understand, relate to, and appreciate. For instance, if you're talking about the advantages of public speaking to a group of Asian immigrants, who may be reluctant to speak, you could adapt your information and show how effective presentational skills can be desirable in job interviews, work performance, and academic success.

Transitions within the Body of the Speech

Now that you have your main points selected and developed with supporting material, you will need to move your listeners smoothly from one point to the next. Although there are numerous transitions available to serve this function, numbered transitions are the simplest and most informative type to use.

The *numbered transition* is a sentence stating which main point you will be presenting and its content. For instance, "The first characteristic of a good marriage is open communication" or "The third and final step in negotiation is the closing phase."

The numbered transition is useful because it tells the audience not only what you will be speaking of next but also where you are in the speech. This type of "signposting" encourages the audience to pay closer attention to what is being said and helps them retain the information.

A second technique that really helps the audience move from one point to another is a moment of *silence* before you state your numbered transition. A two- or three-second pause between the last word of your preceding main point and your numbered transition serves as a welcome rest for your audience to digest what has been said.

After you end your introduction or one of your main points in the body of the speech, simply stop with a *two-* or *three-second pause* (one thousand one…, one thousand two…, one thousand three) and then proceed to your numbered transition. The use of pauses is a dramatic and visible sign of speaker confidence. Use the two- or three-second pause. It gives you time to breathe, focus, and relax. We should pause more in our daily lives too.

THE INTRODUCTION

Once the body of the speech is completed, you can begin working on the introduction. The introduction serves two primary functions. First, it captures the attention of the audience with an attention getter. Second, it previews the main points you will be presenting in the body of the speech. The introduction should take no more than 10 to 15 percent of the total speaking time.

The Attention Getter

The first objective of the introduction is to *capture the attention of the audience*. This can be accomplished by any number of attention getters, such as an audience question, an amusing anecdote, a startling statement, a startling statistic, a hypothetical situation, a quotation, or a joke. No matter which attention getter you choose, it should relate directly to the topic you will be presenting, and it should appropriately match the overall tone of your speech. You wouldn't want to begin a serious speech with a joke, nor would you start a humorous speech with a sad anecdote. Let's take a look at an example of each attention getter.

Audience Question
"How many of you have ever danced with a brown bear, ridden sidesaddle on a horse, or jumped through a burning hoop? Well, I have. And today, I'd like to speak about my career in the circus."

Amusing Anecdote
"Two monks were walking toward a stream when they were approached by a beautiful woman. She asked if they could help her cross the swiftly

moving water. The older monk agreed to help. He then carried the woman across the stream in his arms and let her go on the other side.

"As the two monks continued their journey for some time, the younger monk turned and asked the older monk, 'Why did you carry that woman across the stream? You know our vows don't permit us to touch women.'

"'I carried the woman across the river, that is true,' replied the older monk. 'But I let her go when we got to the other side. It seems that you are still carrying her.' Today, I am going to talk about letting go of past hurts.'"

Startling Statement
"More individuals are murdered by people they know than by complete strangers. Although this may seem unbelievable, this statement is none-theless true. Today, I am going to talk about murder in the United States."

Startling Statistic
"In 1998, teachers in Japan ranked in the top 15 percent of all wage earn-ers in that island nation. Today, I'd like to talk about the salaries of teachers in the United States."

Hypothetical Situation
"Imagine yourself sitting on a warm, sandy beach in Hawaii. You can see the deep blue sea stretching out to the horizon. You can hear the waves in the distance, and the smell of the late afternoon ocean breeze sur-rounds you. A relaxed, wonderful feeling engulfs you. Stay there for a moment. Today, I'd like to share with you some highlights of my last trip to Hawaii."

Quotation
"Psychotherapist Heinz Kohut once said, 'The ability to soothe your own soul in the face of adversity is the most powerful skill you can develop in your lifetime.' Today, I'd like to speak about the benefits of positive self-talk."

Joke
"One of my problems is that I internalize everything. I can't express my anger, so I grow a tumor instead. Well, maybe I'm stretching the truth a bit, but I do have difficulty expressing anger. Today, I want to talk about the hazards of not expressing your anger."

There are many other attention getters you might consider as you construct your introduction. Other methods include referring to the occasion, referring to the previous speaker, building up suspense, using a visual aid, establishing common ground with the audience, pointing to an historical event, complimenting the audience, and stressing the importance of the speech topic. Remember that whatever attention getter you decide on, it should relate directly to the topic, and it should appropriately match the overall tone of the speech. Keep your attention getters relatively short, because the entire introduction should comprise only 10 to 15 percent of your total speaking time.

Preview of Main Points

After you have given your attention getter, you should pause for one or two seconds, then present your preview of main points. The purpose of the preview of main points is to give your audience a foreshadowing of what's to follow in the speech. It prepares their minds to receive the points you will be speaking on. The preview of points should be only one sentence in length. A common mistake is to say too much in the preview, almost giving a minispeech for each point previewed. Keep it brief and to the point. Only one sentence! Here are some examples of acceptable previews of main points:

> "The three steps to making cookies are gathering your materials, preparing your ingredients, and, finally, baking the cookies."
>
> "The three parts of the guitar are the head, neck, and body."
>
> "Running can improve your physical stamina, reduce psychological stress, and increase your spiritual awareness."
>
> "The three components of a healthy relationship are caring, communication, and companionship."

After you've given the preview of main points, pause for one or two seconds before you state your first numbered transition. This pause will give your audience time to digest the preview of points.

THE CONCLUSION

After you have finished your final point in the body of the speech, it is important to have a two- or three-second pause *before* you begin your conclusion. Actually say to yourself silently "one thousand one…, one thousand two…, one thousand three" before you start your conclusion. This brief pause will let your audience know that you will be ending shortly.

The first words out of your mouth during the conclusion will be your summary of main points. Please don't say, "In conclusion…," or "I guess it's time for me to quit," or "Well, I'd better end now." Those transitions into the conclusion are unnecessary and awkward.

Your conclusion should summarize your main points in one sentence and leave your audience with a final thought or appeal. The conclusion should require only 5 to 10 percent of your total speaking time. In a five-minute speech, that's approximately 15 to 30 seconds. That might not sound like a great deal of time, but it will be sufficient to summarize your points and leave the audience with a final thought or appeal.

Summary of Main Points

The summary of main points should be a *one-sentence* review of the three or four points you presented in your speech. One simple sentence will do. Nothing more. Here are some examples of main-point summaries:

"Today I've shared the three steps to making cookies: gathering your materials, preparing your ingredients, and, finally, baking the cookies."

"In my talk this morning, I described the head, the neck, and the body of the guitar."

"So remember, running can improve physical stamina, reduce psychological stress, and increase your spiritual awareness."

"Today I spoke about the three components of a healthy relationship, which are caring, communication, and companionship."

Final Thought or Appeal

After you have summarized your points, it's best to leave your audience with one final thought. This thought can be a return to your attention getter, an appeal, a quotation, a vision for the future, or a call to action. The final thought shouldn't be very long. Present a concise and focused thought for your audience to remember. This is not the time to begin another main point. Here are some examples of the various methods:

Return to attention getter. "Like the young man in my opening story who wanted to know the secret of living a long life, I hope you will examine your life and attempt to reduce the stresses in it."

Appeal. "As we have seen, drug use among our teenagers is at a record high, and many of us adults have been denying its existence. Our denial will not rid us of the drugs. Our denial will not put the drug dealers in prison. Our denial will not save our children's lives. It's time that we opened our eyes and began thinking about the horrors of teenage drug use."

Quotation. "John Steinbeck once observed, 'A marriage is like a journey. The certain way to be wrong is to think you control it.' I hope that you will relax a little more in your marriage or in your relationships in the future, and follow the guidelines I've outlined this morning on how to give your spouse more personal space."

Vision for the future. "I see a future for our club with 1,000 members, not just 28. I see a future in which our club will donate thousands of dollars to local charities, not just $200. Our club will be a place for all women of Oakland to meet, build lasting friendships, and most important, give something back to the community that provided us with our beginning. Do you see this vision also?"

Call to action. "The election is two weeks away. If you share my beliefs for a strong America, if you share my desire for a prosperous America, if you share my dream for a free America, I ask you to invest in the future of our great land. I ask you to contribute just $100 to my campaign fund this very morning. My assistants will be distributing the contribution forms to you in a few moments."

Don't feel limited to these final-thought devices. You can use a combination of two of them, or make up your own final statement format. Remember to keep the final thought short and to the point, however. Don't ramble. Your final thought shouldn't be longer than 30 seconds for a five-minute speech.

Once you have completed your final thought, smile and pause for two or three seconds, then walk back to your seat. If you are permitted a question-and-answer period, remain at the podium and wait for the applause to end. Once the applause has ceased, pause a second or two, then request questions from your audience. In either case, the pauses are very important. It shows your audience that you are in control.

CONSTRUCTING YOUR SPEECH OUTLINE

Now that we have introduced the various components of the introduction, body, and conclusion, we need to spend a few moments reviewing some guidelines for writing a speech outline. Although some professional speakers do not use any outline in the preparation of their talks, they are few in number. The majority of speakers, both beginning and professional, use some form of outlining to help them plan and test their speech ahead of time. The outline is your most important tool in constructing a well-developed and easy-to-follow speech.

The *speech outline* is a short, complete-sentence model of your speech. From this outline, you can test the organization, logic, and development of your entire speech. The total number of words in your outline shouldn't exceed 30 percent of the actual number of spoken words in your speech.

Here are some guidelines that will assist you in your construction of a speech outline:

Use a standard set of symbols. As you organize the body of your speech, use a standard set of symbols. The main points of the speech will be divided by Roman numerals (I, II, III), subpoints will be designated by capital letters (A, B, C), and minor headings will be designated by Arabic numerals (1, 2, 3).

Use complete-sentence structure for major headings. Complete-sentence structure for your major headings will help test the logic and development of your speech structure. Although you can use a key-word-outline note card when you deliver your speech, a full-sentence outline will permit an analysis of your main- and subpoint structure.

Each main point should reinforce or clarify your specific purpose statement. This is one of the most important tests of your speech outline. Does each main point actually develop your specific purpose statement by reinforcing or clarifying it? If a main point does not, it should not be included in your speech.

Each main point and subpoint should contain only one idea. If a main point or subpoint contains more than a single thought or idea, it will confuse you and your audience. The logic of your speech structure is weakened when you present multiple ideas in a main point or subpoint. If you see an "and" in one of your main-point or subpoint headings, you will need to decide on one of the two ideas to present, or you can split them into two headings if it's appropriate. For example:

II. The second advantage that jogging offers is that it increases your physical endurance *and* your psychological well-being. (Incorrect—Notice the "and" in the sentence? Let's change it.)

II. The second advantage that jogging offers is that it increases your physical endurance.

III. The third advantage that jogging offers is that it increases your sense of psychological well-being.

Subpoints should support main points. Check to make sure that not only do your main points support your specific purpose statement, but your subpoints support your main points as well. This is called *subordination of points.* Each subpoint should be directly related to the main point it falls under. If not, it needs to go. For example:

II. The second floor of City Hall houses the city officials.
   A. The mayor is located in the west wing of the second floor.
   B. The city manager is located next to the mayor.
   C. *The city records are located on the third floor.*
   (Point "C" does not relate directly to the main point. It needs to be placed under another main-point heading that deals with the third floor.)

Limit your main points to a maximum of four. Don't overburden your audience with too many main points. The average listener cannot remember more than three or four main points, regardless of the length of the speech. Three main points are usually your best bet for any speech.

Write the introduction and conclusion word for word. Because the introduction is so important in capturing the attention of the audience and the conclusion needs to bring your speech to a concise ending, there is little room for ad-libbing or impromptu speaking. Therefore, your introduction and conclusion should be written out verbatim in the outline.

Limit the outline to 30 percent of the total speech wording. The entire number of words in your outline, introduction, and conclusion, should not exceed 30 percent of your total speaking words. More than 30 percent will make your outline resemble a manuscript speech, and your final presentation will run the risk of having a manuscript or memorized delivery style.

On the following page is a sample outline of a tribute speech. Notice the various components of the speech—the specific purpose, introduction, body, and conclusion. We will include a bibliography in later outline samples, but for now, just notice the overall structure of an outline. Let's keep it simple for now.

Sample Outline

A Tribute to George McClendon

Specific Purpose: To pay tribute to George McClendon.

Introduction

Have you ever spent a weekend with a Trappist monk who runs marathons? Well, I have! Today, I'd like to tell you about a man who influenced my life in a significant way. His name is George McClendon. George is a practicing Gestalt therapist in Watsonville, and I met him two summers ago when I was enrolled in one of his U.C. Extension courses. I'd like to tell you about his wonderful relationship workshops, his 20-year career as a Trappist monk, and his marathon running.

Body

    I. *The first thing I want to share with you is that George McClendon teaches excellent relationship workshops.*
   - **A.** His weekend relationship workshops for counselors emphasize a Gestalt approach to systems theory.
   - **B.** George conducts his workshops with wisdom and empathy.

    II. *The second thing I want to share is George's 20-year career as a Trappist monk.*
   - **A.** George spent 20 years in an Oklahoma Trappist monastery.
   - **B.** He helped build the monastery from the foundation to the roof.

    III. *The final thing I want to tell you about is George's newfound interest in marathon running.*
   - **A.** At age 53, he began jogging as a part-time hobby.
   - **B.** Six months later he completed the Big Sur Marathon.

Conclusion

Today, I've talked about George McClendon's relationship workshops, his life as a monk, and his marathon running. He is truly an inspiring individual who has taught me to appreciate life and dream big dreams. I hope you get a chance to meet him.

COMMUNICATION ACTIVITIES

Personal Activities

1. **Simplifying your life**

   Make a list of all the duties, responsibilities, and chores you have to complete in the next week. Write down everything, from going to that job interview to feeding the cats. Your list should be substantial. Now, circle the three tasks that are the most important—if you couldn't do any of the others, these are the top three you would need to complete. Now, underline the next three most important tasks. Don't cheat, only three of them! Cross out the remaining tasks. That's right, you have only six tasks you can do. The rest will go uncompleted, at least for the week. How would your life change if you could do only these six things? How do you feel? What would your week be like? On the day you die, you will leave one hundred things undone.

2. **Soothing the many sides of you**

   Get a piece of typing paper (or any 8½ × 11-inch paper) and fold it into thirds. Label one column "BODY," the middle column "MIND," and the third column "SPIRIT." For each column, take a few minutes to brainstorm a list of activities that you enjoy or find rewarding. For example, for "BODY" you might include bathing, eating, playing in the sand, flossing, stretching, and skipping pebbles on water. Do this for each column. Look at your lists. How does each feel? Have you done any of these activities lately? If not, which ones could you do today?

3. **Organizing thoughts in other cultures**

   Ask an individual from a different culture how important the concept of clear, logical thought patterns is to him or her. Does she or he value critical thinking? How does this person feel about our emphasis on clear organizational patterns in speech construction? What forms of oral discourse or presentation are emphasized in their culture, if any?

Class Activities

1. **Group discussion: Five words or less**

   Divide the class into groups of five or six. Each group is to discuss for 10 minutes some aspect of communication suggested by the instructor. Students are free to express their thoughts and feelings, except each person is not permitted to use more than five words during any given opportunity to address the group. No more than five words at a time. It's helpful in this exercise to count each of your five words on your fingers. This will give you a good feel for each word that comes out of your mouth. How does this way of talking feel to you? How do the other group members feel? Did you notice any communication interaction changes because of this limit? This may be the first time you have ever valued the currency of your language. Remember, the more you say, the less you say. And the less you say, the more you say. Be prepared to discuss your reactions to this activity in class.

2. **Three highlights of your life speech**

    Construct a formal outline detailing the speech topic (specific purpose), "To inform the audience of the three highlights of my life." Remember to have supporting material in the subpoints of the speech. Prepare, practice, and present a three-to-five-minute informative speech. Your speech should contain an introduction, body, and conclusion.

3. **The three sides of me speech**

    Prepare, practice, and present a three-to-five-minute speech about interesting aspects of your physical, intellectual, and spiritual self. Review Personal Activity 2 in this chapter to get some ideas on how to develop your points. Your speech should contain an introduction, body, and conclusion.

7

DELIVERING YOUR SPEECH
Being Yourself

Mike enrolled in a public speaking course during his first quarter at the University of California at Santa Barbara. As a first-quarter freshman, he was surprised to discover that the vast majority of students in the class were seniors who had avoided the public speaking course until their final year of college.

There was one senior in the class named Ron, who spoke with authority. Mike would sit mesmerized by the sound of this voice. Ron would stand behind the podium, almost motionless, with only the slightest twist of the wrist or a subtle tilting of his head to accentuate a point or ease the audience into his next thought. What confidence! What command! Mike now had a role model for speaking.

As he practiced his third speech of the course, Mike literally spent hours trying to lower his voice to match Ron's deep, resonant musical notes. As he practiced his talk, his body wanted to dance, as it had during the first two speeches, but Mike restricted his movements, so he could match Ron's subtle and almost aloof gestures and posturing. As he practiced, Mike became more and more excited. His practice was paying off. He was speaking and moving just like Ron. It was working.

Mike's third speech, however, was a bomb. He didn't really know what had happened that morning in class when he got up to speak. His voice was deep like Ron's. His posture was motionless like Ron's. And his gestures were as subtle as any Ron had presented. In fact, Mike felt like he was Ron! But something wasn't right.

It wasn't until after class that Michelle, one of the other students, came up to Mike in the hallway and said, "I liked the 'friendly' Mike more." That's all she had to say. Michelle liked the "friendly" Mike more. She liked the old Mike, and not his imitation of Ron.

Mike took Michelle's comment to heart, and two weeks later he delivered his next speech in a more relaxed and conversational tone of voice. He talked and moved naturally. He was being himself, and not acting like somebody else. And it felt right. This was one of the most important lessons Mike learned in his public speaking class—to be himself by speaking naturally.

CHARACTERISTICS OF GOOD DELIVERY

The content of your speech is what you say. Your delivery is how you say it. It's the overall "who" that you present to the audience, not the "what" you say. Delivery is more than just the volume, rate, pitch, and enunciation of your voice. It includes your appearance, posture, body movement, hand gestures, eye contact, and facial expressions. In other words, *delivery is all of the nonverbal communication you express to your audience when you speak.*

The old adage "It's not what you say, but how you say it" merits serious reflection, especially in light of current research. Studies have shown that nonverbal communication has a greater impact than verbal communication when we receive and interpret messages. One such study asserts that only 7 percent of our emotional response to another person is determined by the verbal component of what is said, while 93 percent of our response is shaped by the speaker's nonverbal behavior![1]

What does this mean to you as a public speaker? Obviously, it suggests plenty. The most thoroughly researched and well-organized speech will have little impact on an audience if the speaker's delivery lacks a conversational quality, a sense of communication, and speaker naturalness.

Enlarged Conversational Quality

The majority of impressive professional speakers you have observed in person or heard on radio or television were speakers who probably sounded more like formal orators whose voices boomed rather than whispered, whose gestures painted grandiose scenes, and whose bodies illustrated every phrase. Often these speakers were addressing large audiences, and such delivery might have been appropriate for the occasion. But for our public speaking purposes, the most effective speaking style is an enlarged conversational quality.

An *enlarged conversational quality* of speaking means talking with the same naturalness and quality of voice you would use when speaking with another person, only enlarged just a little. To do this, you increase the volume of your conversational tone of voice so people in the back of the room can hear you, and you expand your gestures and movements a bit so all the audience can see them. The primary goal of using an enlarged conversational quality is that your audience will get the feeling that you are talking to them in a natural fashion, not talking at them with calculated and rehearsed gestures.

How can you speak with an enlarged conversational quality when your body stiffens, your hands freeze, and your voice tightens even at the thought of addressing an audience? The most useful way to achieve this enlarged conversational quality while planning and practicing your speech is to imagine that you are talking to just *one* person.

See this person in your mind's eye as you prepare the wording of your outline and practice the delivery of your talk. Try practicing your speech with the mental image of someone you feel safe with. You don't need a photograph of the individual, just the mental image. If you can do this successfully, you will begin to acquire the correct conversational tone.

Sense of Communication

It's been referred to as "speaker directness," "speaker presence," "focus," "love for the audience," and "immediacy." We'll simply refer to it as the speaker's *sense of communication*. This sense of communication is the feeling the audience senses when a speaker really wants to be there sharing her message. The audience knows the speaker really desires to communicate with them. She wants to be there, and not somewhere else. The speaker is not forced to talk; she wants to talk.

With a sense of communication, the speaker also communicates an awareness of and a sensitivity to her audience. The speaker's eyes are focused on the audience, not on the notes. She is aware of the audience's feedback, sensitive to their responses. They get the sense that she sees them, feels them, is with them in body and spirit.

This sounds like a description of the behavior of someone who loves you—the immediacy, the focus, the concern, and the sensitivity. No, you're not required to fall in love with your audience; however, you are encouraged to forget yourself and focus your attention, your thinking, and your energy on being there with your audience, showing your desire to communicate with them.

Emerson once warned, "Who you are speaks so loudly, I can't hear your words anymore." Hopefully, you are a speaker who wants to be there sharing with the audience. They will soon forget most of your words, but they will remember you and your desire to communicate.

Speaker Naturalness

There's an old Jewish proverb that wisely asks the question, "If you can't be yourself, who can you be?" A common and disturbing problem that prevents us from living a free and healthy life is our inclination to try to act, think, and be like someone else—awkward attempts to be someone we are not. Granted, imitation is one of the basic tools in learning, whether for language acquisition or writing style. But as a template for living, it can be hazardous.

When Mike was trying to imitate Ron, he was uncomfortable and awkward. For 18 years Mike had spoken like Mike. He had talked and behaved in a manner that was natural for him, and no one else. Mike was comfortable with the way he communicated. His voice may not have been as deep as Ron's, but it was friendly and warm. His gestures may not have been as smooth as Ron's, but they were expressive. And his body movement wasn't as controlled as Ron's, but it showed his enthusiasm and desire to communicate.

Over the years, Mike has improved the quality of his voice, the smoothness of his gestures, and the movement of his body. And so will you. But Mike's fundamentally the same speaker he was back then. The big difference now is that Mike has come to appreciate and develop his own natural speaking style. He isn't trying to be someone else. And neither should you.

No one else in the world speaks exactly as you do. And no one else in the world feels, acts, or thinks exactly as you do either. Your individuality is what makes you, you. That's what makes life so stimulating and exciting—the differences, not the similarities. Perhaps your individuality or naturalness is the most "precious possession" you can share with another person.

As you speak to your audience, let them see the real you. Don't hide behind the voice of someone else. Don't disguise the rhythms of your gestures. And don't conceal your body's true dance. The audience has you for only a few minutes of their lives; let them hear the real you, not someone else.

"If you can't be yourself, who can you be?"

ELEMENTS OF GOOD DELIVERY

Now that we've examined the three characteristics of good delivery, we can look at its specific elements. Those elements include your body, gestures, eye contact, facial expressions, breathing, and vocal characteristics.

Body

Your body communicates a great deal about you to others. The first thing your audience will notice about you is your overall appearance as you step up to the podium or take center stage. Your appearance in terms of dress and grooming will have a significant impact on an audience.

A speaker's attire can enhance or detract from the effectiveness of the presentation. Somewhat formal dress can often increase a speaker's credibility with an audience, whereas flamboyant, shabby, or enticing attire can actually distract, annoy, and even anger the audience. You don't necessarily have to suit up in a tux or evening gown, but you should carefully and thoughtfully consider the audience and the occasion, and dress accordingly. This is not the time to dig into your car trunk and throw on your cutoffs, dirty beach T-shirt, and rubber thongs.

Grooming should also be an important consideration when preparing for your talk. A hot shower and a splash of cologne or perfume will not only enhance your appearance but also make you feel better about yourself.

Once you're up there at the podium, your audience will check out your overall *posture.* Before you begin speaking, *pause at least three seconds to center your weight evenly on your two feet.* Don't lean on one foot more than the other. Equal weight, that's what we want here. And your feet should not be spread more than shoulder width. A little less would be fine. Keep your back straight, and square your shoulders to the audience. Don't aim a shoulder at the audience—square those shoulders.

Let your hands hang at your sides freely as you take your three-second pause before speaking. A common error made by novice speakers is that they don't pause and get set before speaking. They simply run up and begin talking nervously even before they reach the podium. That sends a loud message to the audience. It says the speaker is nervous, anxious, and literally out of control. Take those three seconds to center yourself. It will pay off for the remainder of your talk.

When an individual faces an audience, the normal response is to freeze. Not move. But a rigid, motionless delivery style would be monotonous to watch for even a short period of time; and it will only serve to make you, the speaker, more tense and nervous. *Body movement* has been shown to attract the attention of an audience. You don't need to do cartwheels across the stage or backflips off the podium, but there are some body movements that are helpful in sustaining audience interest and emphasizing important points.

Speaking of podiums, try moving away and speaking from the side of the podium to communicate a more informal speaking style. This more informal and natural speaking style is beneficial in most speaking situations. If the audience can hear your voice without the use of the podium microphone, step away from the podium when you're speaking. This will give you more room for body movement and gestures.

You might also find it useful to walk two or three short steps to your right or left when you state a main-point transition or stress an important phrase in your talk. That's called *walking into your points*. This walking movement recaptures the audience's attention and visually reinforces the transition from one point to another. Walk slowly when you do this. Don't rush. Stroll slowly into your next point.

If you want to get more intimate with your audience, walk a few steps in their direction. Be careful not to fall off the stage, but stroll toward the audience. This movement works really well when you're giving the punch line to a joke or the climactic ending to a story. You can do just the opposite, that is, walk away from the audience, when you want to voice strong emotion. Just a few steps back is all you need.

A final word on body movement. Too much movement, unrelated movement, or repetitious movement can be distracting to an audience. Use your body movement to direct attention and emphasize points during your talk. Use it carefully.

Gestures

Your *gestures* consist of your hand and arm movements during your speech. Use your gestures to emphasize and express important ideas and emotions. The normal tendency for a beginning speaker, when facing an audience, is to cement her hands to the sides of the podium, clutch her hands either in front or in back of herself, or freeze them at her sides. This too can only serve to increase the speaker's anxiety. There are two excellent practice techniques you can use to loosen up your hands and arms.

The first one we'll call the *silent hula technique*. Just as a Hawaiian hula dancer does, you can practice communicating passages or sections of your speech *without words,* using only your hands and arms to express the thoughts and feelings. Sounds silly, but it gets your mind off the words of the speech and refocuses your attention on your gestures. You'll be pleasantly surprised at how your hands come alive once you forget about the words and concentrate on the message.

The second technique for loosening up your hands and arms is called *catching rain*. Catching rain is exactly what it sounds like. You stand with both hands comfortably outstretched in front of you, with elbows at your sides. Then begin to recite your speech. The only rule with this practice technique is that your hands and arms cannot fall beneath your waist. That's the only rule. As you speak, you will notice your arms will begin to move by themselves as you talk! It's like they have a life all their own. Small movements at first, but then more pronounced as you get into your talk. Who knows why it works. But once your mind is occupied with your mental chatter, it forgets about the hands and arms, and the body takes over. Sounds weird. But give it a try.

Eye Contact

The manner in which eye-contact behavior is interpreted varies from culture to culture. But in the American culture, you are expected to have direct eye contact if you are to be perceived as interested, honest, and credible. If not, you run the risk of being seen as uninterested, reticent, or even devious. When you speak to an audience, this principle holds true also.

Direct eye contact with your audience serves a variety of positive functions for the speaker. First, it establishes contact with the audience. How can a relationship be established if you don't even see them? Second, eye contact holds the attention of the audience. You don't need to look into the eyes of every one of your audience members to keep their attention, but spread your eye contact around the room. Look at the front, the back, and the sides. Don't get stuck on one section of the room. Avoid looking at your notes, the floor, or the ceiling. Third, eye contact is the best way to receive feedback from the audience. Do they look bored? Are they interested? Are they confused? All these questions can be answered quickly and silently by glancing around the room. Finally, eye contact suggests honesty. The old adage "A person won't look you in the eye if they're lying" seems to be true in public speaking as well.

Facial Expressions

Once a relationship has been established, research has found that the face is the area at which most people look to observe and evaluate the emotional responses of another person. As a public speaker, your facial expressions are important in your communication. Although many of the audience members in the back rows will not be able to see your expressions in detail, all of your listeners will develop a sense of how you are feeling and who you are by your facial cues. In addition to your eye-contact behavior, your ability to use your mouth and face to emphasize, stress, and illustrate emotions cannot be overlooked.

Facial expressions and habits are one of the most difficult movements to change or modify, primarily because we are so unaware of them. Like the sound of our voice, our facial expressions have a life all their own, outside of our conscious awareness. We simply cannot see our face as we go about our daily life. Sure, we can view it in a mirror, a photograph, or even on videotape, but those are indeed brief moments. So, our faces are literally strangers to us.

If you want to try something really unusual, stare at your face in a mirror for five minutes without looking away. No distractions. No one else in the room. Just look at your own face for five minutes. See what happens. The image in the mirror becomes almost unrecognizable after a few moments of studying the detail of your own face. Who are you, anyway?

Here's one specific suggestion for your facial expressions while you give your speech. Smile. This suggestion may sound trite, and yet it needs repeating. You need to smile. Did you know it takes less muscle effort to smile than to frown? No wonder we get so exhausted when we're frowning during our bad moods.

Smile during the first three seconds you're in front of your audience, as you get your posture centered. Even if you are going to present a very somber topic, you can still invest three seconds for smiling. It'll relax both you and your audience. You'll discover when you smile during this initial phase of the speech that you're more likely to loosen up and express a variety of emotions during the remainder of your talk.

But what if you're not a smiler by nature, or you happen to be depressed that day? Fake it! Yeah, fake it! Life's too short. You owe it to your audience to be "up" for your talk. You can frown for the rest of the day. But give your audience the best you have. This is not therapy; it's your speech, your gift to the audience. Make it a good one!

Breathing

An entire book could be written on the importance of breathing, but we're going to spend only three paragraphs stressing its pivotal role in making you an effective speaker. For starters, if you didn't breathe once during a five-minute speech, you'd most likely pass out, and maybe even die. How about that for being important? You could go through an entire five-minute talk and never once look at one person, give one gesture, state one transition, or wear a stitch of clothing, and not much would happen to you. Maybe speaking naked would cause something to happen, but overall, nothing much would. Yet, without breathing for those five minutes, you die. That simple.

More than 2,000 years ago, Lao Tzu said, "It is not wise to rush about. Controlling the breath causes strain." Did you know that when you're frightened or anxious, you hold your breath? When you're speaking before an audience, you have a tendency to hold your breath. You see it in just about every beginning speaker. The rapid rate of speech. The run-on sentences, punctuated occasionally by huge gulps of air. Remember, even when you're under extreme stress, your body knows enough not to kill itself.

What can you do to breathe properly when speaking to an audience? Three things, really. First, begin breathing in deep, even breaths about a minute or two before you are called to speak. Don't hyperventilate and pass out. Just slow, deep, even breaths. Second, while you're smiling and centering your posture during the first three seconds in front of your audience, draw in three deep breaths while you're doing your "one thousand one..., one thousand two..., one thousand three." This will give you air to begin your speech. Third, breathe after each long sentence during your speech. Breathe from the stomach, not from the throat. Inhale with your stomach. Pause often in your speech. Pause long enough to inhale deeply and exhale completely. This will seem like an eternity when you're up in front of all those people, but it will save you. It will save not only your life but your speaking style as well.

Vocal Characteristics

There are six aspects of your voice worth mentioning here. Your vocal characteristics are made up of rate, volume, pitch, inflection, enunciation, and vocal variety.

Your speaking *rate* is the speed at which you talk. It's generally measured in number of words per minute. The average speaking rate is about 110 to 130 words per minute. Some people speak more slowly, some faster. If you speak too slowly, you run the risk of losing the attention of your audience. If you speak too quickly, you make it difficult for your audience to understand you. In addition, an extremely rapid rate of speech can annoy or irritate an audience. Find a rate of speech that is comfortable for you, but don't feel that it is best to stick to this speed. One of the marks of an experienced speaker is the ability to vary the speaking rate. The most common error is for the beginning speaker to speak too rapidly. In that case, you should pause more after long sentences and phrases, and take deep breaths. Another helpful aid is to occasionally mark in red the word "SLOW" on your note cards.

Volume is the loudness of your voice. In public speaking, you have to speak loudly enough so that your listeners in the back row can hear you without straining. If the people in the back appear to be having difficulty, stop your talk and ask them if your voice can be heard. Speak louder if they can't hear you. A soft voice not only makes it difficult for the audience to listen to your speech, it also can be interpreted as a sign of reticence, weakness, or fear.

If you discover that you need to develop more volume in your speaking, you might try practicing the *backyard yelling exercise*. You'll need a friend for this one. Anyone will do. Have your assistant sit in a chair in the backyard, in the parking lot of your apartment house, or anywhere you have 30 feet of free space where you won't get hit by traffic. Pace off about 30 feet between you and your assistant. Begin your speech. If your friend cannot hear you, have him raise his hand for you to increase your volume. Increase your volume, even if you feel as if you're screaming. Your assistant will lower his hand when he can hear you. This goes back and forth until you reach a volume that is loud enough for your assistant to hear from 30 feet. If you can pass this test, you'll be heard in any room.

Pitch refers to the highness or lowness of your voice. It can be thought of as the placement of your voice on a musical scale. Each individual has a natural pitch level. The movement of pitch either upward or downward from this natural pitch level is known as *inflection*. Inflection is used to give certain words or phrases emphasis. A speaker who never varies her pitch (inflection) is said to speak in a monotone fashion. A monotone voice is a boring voice after a few minutes.

One way to get inflection into your voice is to emphasize important words in your sentences. Read aloud the sentence that follows while emphasizing a different word with each reading. Begin with the emphasis on the first word, and read the sentence. Then read the sentence again, with the emphasis on the second word. Repeat the process until you've read through the sentence seven times.

I would love to see you again.

The meaning of the sentence changes with each different reading, doesn't it? Inflection is a powerful verbal tool in speech emphasis, and it is one of the most effective cures for a monotone delivery.

One last method for changing the monotone voice is called the *singing exercise*. You simply sing your words as you practice your speech. In a standing position, deliver your speech by singing every word. Make up a melody as you go along. Don't sing to the melody of a song you know. Just let the words and melody flow. It may feel foolish initially, but who cares? The point is to break your monotone habit.

Enunciation consists of articulation and pronunciation. *Articulation* is defined as the ability to pronounce the letters of a word correctly, whereas *pronunciation* is the ability to pronounce the entire word correctly. There are three common causes of articulation problems: sound substitution, slurring, and the omission of sounds.

Sound substitution happens often in speaking. Many of us say "budder" instead of "butter," or "dat" instead of "that." In the first case, we substituted the sound of "d" for "t," and in the second example, we substituted the sound of "d" for "th."

Slurring is usually caused by a rapid rate of speech or a running together of words. We often say "I'll getcha a hot dog," instead of "I will get you a hot dog." Be aware of slurring your words when you speak.

The final cause of articulation problems is the *omission of sounds*. We sometimes say "flowin'" instead of "flowing," or "singin'" instead of "singing." Don't get lazy when you pronounce your words.

The final characteristic of your voice is *vocal variety*. Vocal variety refers to the variance or range you give to the rate, volume, and pitch of your speech. You'll recall that inflection is the variance or change in pitch. This gives your voice vocal variety. Variance in your volume and rate also plays an important role in keeping your speech interesting and lively. Vocal variety in your pitch, volume, and rate prevents a monotone speech delivery, and nothing puts your audience to sleep faster than a monotone voice.

SPEECH PRACTICE

No one is born with public speaking skills, no matter what you think. The outstanding speakers are those individuals who invest countless hours of practice time improving their skills. Nothing comes without a price.

This book isn't worth a penny if you don't actually take the time and effort to practice the skills that we have been discussing up to now. The choice is ultimately yours. It's always yours. When you practice your speech, consider these guidelines for a productive practice session.

Complete Your Outline before You Practice
Begin your practice sessions only after you have typed your final outline. Read through your outline a number of times so you become familiar with the content and structure. Then make your 4 × 6-inch note card of main points and key words so you can quickly refer to it during your practice sessions.

Choose a Private Practice Site
Select a room in your house, apartment, or yacht that will give you adequate space to walk three or four steps in any direction. Don't practice in your car during a rush-hour commute. Select a real room that is free of interruptions and distractions, such as telephones, children running through, a noisy television, or even Grandma knitting quietly in the corner next to the laser disc unit. After you've selected the room, set up three chairs, side by side, to represent your audience. You should be standing about eight feet away from the chairs, facing in their direction. Remember to have about three or four steps of clear space all around you so you can walk into your transitions.

Practice in a Standing Position
There are people who practice their speeches in a prone position, in a sitting position, and even in the lotus position. But you will be standing when you deliver your speech to your audience, so you should be standing when you are practicing. If you won't practice from a standing posi-

tion, you might as well just squirt lighter fluid on this book right now and set a match to it. Make sure you burn it in a safe place, however, like the fireplace. Please practice your speech in a standing position. Anything short of this is a sin.

Loosen Up before You Begin Practicing

As you stare at the three chairs representing your audience, get a mental picture of one of your favorite people in the world sitting in the chair on your left. Don't worry about the chair on your right. As you visualize that person, begin your deep breathing. Breathe for a minute or two with your eyes open. Deep, even breaths from your stomach. Shake your hands vigorously at your sides. Keep breathing. Roll your head to the right a couple of times, then to the left a few more times. Sing a song or just talk gibberish for a minute or so, starting out with a low volume, then going up in volume until you almost reach a shouting intensity. Keep this up until you feel like you're loose and ready to go.

Practice in Small Increments Initially

Practice your introduction all the way through two or three times until you get it right. Then move on to your first main point. Practice it by itself two or three times until you're satisfied with your command of the material. Then move on to the second main point. Continue the process until you've completed the conclusion. Just one section at a time. Small increments for now. Once you've moved through the entire speech, section by section, go back to the introduction and first main point, and see if you can get through both of those parts combined. Try it again until you feel satisfied. Then add the second main point to your cluster. Then add the third main point. And finally the conclusion. There, you've got the entire speech.

Time Your Speeches

A stopwatch is a wonderful aid when timing your speeches, but any watch with a sweep second hand will do. Time your small-increment practice sessions. You should be able to figure out roughly how long each section should be. As you practice and check your time, you might have to add a little here and cut a little there. But that's what this is all about. When you are comfortable with each section, time the entire speech and edit your talk so it's within the required time limit. With timed practices, you should know within 30 seconds either way how long your final presentation will be. Now that's preparation!

Practice the Entire Speech Five Times

At one practice session, practice your entire speech two times. A few hours later or the next day, practice your speech another two times all the way through, referring to your note card only when necessary. On the morning you are scheduled to speak, practice your speech only once all the way through. And that's it. No more practice. If you practice your speech too often, you run the risk of sounding memorized. Five times, no more.

Don't Practice in Front of a Mirror
You won't be speaking into a mirror when you deliver your speech, so don't practice with one. Mirrors have a tendency to confuse the speaker. They can distract more than help. So don't even think of practicing in front of one.

Record Your Practice Sessions
If you're really serious about conducting practice sessions that are worthwhile, invest $20 and pick up the cheapest department store audiocassette recorder you can find, and record your five full-speech practice sessions. This takes a little guts and some money, but there's nothing quite like it for evaluating your performance and progress. Don't practice with a videotape unit just yet. It'll overwhelm you with visual stimuli, and you won't be focusing on your speech patterns. Save the videotape for later speeches. For now, just the audiocassette, okay? When listening to your recording, check for naturalness, the desire to communicate, and an enlarged conversational quality. Also check your voice for proper volume, rate, pitch, and vocal variety. Did you have too many verbal pauses, such as "ah," "um," and "you know"? Observe your energy level. Did you sound enthusiastic or dead? See how helpful this $20 recorder can be in your speech practice regimen?

Evaluating Your Speech
Before you deliver your speech to an audience, evaluate one of your practice speeches for content, organization, and delivery. Your practice speech can be videotaped for your viewing, or have a friend watch your practice session. Either way, have your friend or yourself complete the evaluation form on the following page. Don't limit yourself to the objectives contained in the list. Feel free to add your own points. The important thing is for you to critically evaluate your speech before you present it to your audience.

Speech Day Checkout
On the day of your talk, practice your speech one time all the way through. Take a hot shower and dab on your cologne or perfume liberally. Smell good for yourself, if for nobody else. Don't eat a heavy meal or really greasy food three hours before you're scheduled to talk. It'll make you sleepy. And no alcohol anytime before you speak. Arrive early to the auditorium or room, so you can get a feel for the layout, the atmosphere, the podium, and the microphone setup. Also, find out where the

Speaker Evaluation

Content

Topic appropriate to the audience?
Topic specific enough/limited in scope?
Main points adequately developed the speech topic?
Adequate development:
    Human-interest material?
    Statistics/expert testimony?
    Statistics/expert testimony documented?
Vivid, descriptive language?
Visual aids clarified/developed points?
Audience questions answered effectively?

Organization

Introduction:
    Attention getter?
    Purpose of the speech stated?
    Preview of main points?
    Goodwill established?

Body:
    Transitions clearly stated?
    Internal transitions?
    Recap of each point before transition?

Conclusion:
    Summary of main points?
    Final-thought device?

Delivery

Appropriate dress for occasion?
Get set before speaking?
Straight posture?
Relaxed, natural body movement?
Direct eye contact?
Expressive gestures?
Fluid, articulate speech?
Adequate volume?
Adequate vocal variety?

restroom is, a telephone if you need it, and where you will be sitting before you speak. Do all this *before* people begin arriving. As your speaking time nears, try to keep to yourself. This is not the time for idle chit-chat. Keep to yourself, and begin breathing deeply and evenly from your stomach. Glance over your key-word note card once more. Wait quietly until your name is announced. Then slowly get up from your chair, breathing evenly and deeply, as the applause fills your ears. You're now ready to walk to the podium. Aren't you glad you practiced? Have fun. And remember to breathe from the stomach, deeply..., evenly....

Be Gentle on Yourself
No matter what happens—be gentle on yourself. It's only a speech! A hundred years from now, it won't matter all that much. What really counts is your decision to attempt a speech. Go get 'em.

LISTENING TO OTHERS SPEAK

In this chapter, we have discussed ways you can deliver a speech more effectively. And before we move on to informative speaking, we need to briefly examine the other side of public speaking—the listening audience. Without a listening audience, there is no speaker.

The eternal question goes something like this: "If a tree falls in the forest and no one is there to hear it, does it make a sound?" Well, the same question can be asked of public speaking. If a speaker speaks in an auditorium and there are no people in the audience listening (or really paying attention), does the speaker make a sound? A provocative question when you really stop and think about it.

A young psychotherapist, exhausted from listening to clients for eight hours in one day, was walking out to the parking lot of a psychiatric clinic with an older, more experienced therapist. "How is it that you always look so fresh, unburdened, and upbeat at the end of the day?" the young therapist asked of the older therapist. "How can you listen to their problems, hour after hour, day after day, year after year, without having it take its toll on you, like it does me?" The older therapist smiled and replied, "Who listens?"

Hopefully, as audience members, we listen to our speakers the way the younger therapist listens to his patients. Yet it is rare for any audience member to ever receive any training in listening. Therapists train for years and are supervised in counseling sessions for hundreds of hours before they can sit in the counseling room and listen for payment. How can we expect to listen effectively to a speaker without some basic guidelines in listening? Well, here are some hints on listening that might be of help to you when you are asked to listen to a speech.

Listen with Your Presence

Unlike the tree falling in the forest without anyone to hear it crash, you will be in the room listening to the speaker. You need to be present in many ways. First of all, sit near the front of the auditorium or room. If you're going to be there listening, be there. Be present. Sit up near the front of the room. Don't sit in the back. Sitting in the back sends a powerful nonverbal message to the speaker. Especially if the front rows are empty and the back rows are full. How would that make you feel? Now you can understand why some preachers rope off the rear of the church. Second, be there with your entire body. Establish eye contact with the speaker. Smile. If the speaker can see you, wink good luck. That can go a long way to encourage even the most anxious speaker. Don't talk to your neighbor and don't walk out of the room when the speaker is still presenting. Above all, remember to be courteous.

Listen with an Open Mind

Most listening is done through heavy filters or screens of judgment, evaluation, and condemnation. Most of what we hear, we immediately weigh on personal scales of right and wrong, good and bad. We rarely hear what someone has to say. We're much more likely to evaluate whether or not the message is to our liking, whether or not we agree with it, or whether or not we happen to like the speaker's voice, appearance, and mannerisms. We're often very trite and superficial in our listening habits. The first step to listening effectively is to listen with an open mind. We need to consciously remind ourselves of our biases, prejudices, and intolerances as we listen to others and try to be mentally and emotionally spacious with the speaker. We must be open to new ideas, different perspectives, and foreign beliefs. If we constantly build walls of intolerance around us, we soon notice that we are also walled in. We become prisoners of our own closed-mindedness. We need to be open-minded with our speakers.

Listen for the Speaker's Main Ideas

We tend to get caught up in the little things. We get sidetracked, often possessed, by the barking dog next door, the squeak in the dashboard of our new car, and the people talking behind us in the movie theater. The same often holds true for our listening. We get caught up in the sub-points, the minor plots, and we often lose sight of the bigger picture—the main idea of the talk. We need to remember to sit back and listen for the main theme of the speech. We must pay attention to the main ideas the speaker is presenting, and not get sidetracked by all the minor, supporting material. If the speaker is effective, she will repeat the main thesis or proposition of her speech many times throughout the presentation, so listen up. Don't sweat the minutiae—in listening to speeches as well as in life.

Listen for Organizational Patterns

As you listen for the speaker's main ideas and themes, it is often useful to identify the organizational structure of the speech itself. How is the speaker putting this thing together? Is the main-point structure of the talk in topical order, chronological order, spatial order, problem-solution order, and so on? The structure of the main points of the speech will not only enable you to follow the speaker more effectively as she is delivering her talk, but will help you retain the information as well.

Listen with Your Brain

Even though you were asked to listen with an open mind just a few moments ago, you are now being asked to listen critically. Once you have given the speaker's information an open space to enter your brain and exist for a while, you need to eventually do something with that information. Your ability to evaluate the information is a very important responsibility you owe to yourself and the speaker. You need to mentally test the evidence and the reasoning presented by the speaker. Is the evidence from reliable sources? Is there enough evidence to convince you? Is the evidence recent? Is the evidence relevant to the arguments the speaker is proposing? And how about the speaker himself? Does he appear and sound credible? Does the logic of his speech make sense and hold up under analysis? All these things should be examined as you listen to a speech. Listening critically requires an enormous amount of energy and effort. (No wonder the older therapist wasn't exhausted at the end of his day.)

Listen between the Lines

This takes some skill. The ability to listen between the lines is the ability to "hear" or sense what the speaker is attempting to communicate but hasn't actually articulated. Just like the woman who is being asked out for a first date by an inexperienced man who is talking about everything under the sun *except* his invitation to dinner, we need to be able to listen between the lines and hear the real message. Hopefully, as a listener of speeches, you won't be called on to do this often. The speaker should be able to state her theme or main idea clearly and support that theme with adequate material.

Listen with Warmth

As a speaker, you will grow to appreciate and seek out the smiling, nodding, and supportive faces in an audience. As a listener in an audience, you should be as nonverbally supportive of any speaker as you can. This is simply a professional courtesy, from one speaker to another. Perhaps this explains why audiences in public speaking classes are so wonderfully supportive of their speakers. The audience members are themselves speakers, and they know what each speaker is going through. We should all be so lucky as speakers. To listen with warmth, you need to maintain eye contact with the speaker, smile when it's appropriate, nod your head in agreement, and applaud loudly when the speaker is finished. Do unto others....

Listen with Your Heart

Above all, listen with your heart. Give each speaker your most positive, encouraging, and loving feelings as she walks up to the podium. Most members of an audience don't prepare themselves at all before they listen to a speaker. They simply wait for something to come to them—to hit them in the head. They passively wait and receive whatever the speaker has to send. You need to prepare the ground before the speaker says one word. Silently wish the speaker well as she is introduced. Silently encourage the speaker as she begins her talk. Silently affirm her as she delivers her speech. During her conclusion, silently thank her for her efforts and energy. (Think how that would affect all our interpersonal relationships!) Now, the speaker may never know that you were listening with warmth and encouragement, but you will. And that makes all the difference in the world, for you.

Listen with Thanksgiving

Each one of us will have a few regrets on our deathbed. Some of those regrets will involve words of appreciation and thanksgiving that were left unspoken to those who showed us kindness, encouragement, and love during our lifetime. Well, let's finish any "unfinished business." No use your going to your deathbed with a lot of regrets, okay? After a speaker delivers an informative, inspirational, or entertaining speech, you should show your appreciation by thanking her in person after the speaking event is finished. A kind word of thanksgiving and a warm handshake from you might be the only ones the speaker will receive for her efforts. Be that one person. Remember, no regrets.

Listen for the Echoes of Your Own Listening

If you follow these listening guidelines, you will not only be surprised by the improvement in your speech listening skills, you will also be amazed at how much more you will appreciate your own audiences when you speak. The openness, the supportiveness, the caring, and the thanksgiving with which you listen to others will also be mysteriously reflected in the way others listen to you, in your public as well as your private life. You will forever be accompanied by the echoes of your own kindness.

COMMUNICATION ACTIVITIES

Personal Activities

1. **Loosening up**

   Find a large room, an empty meadow, or a deserted beach. Take off your shoes and socks (and anything else you feel comfortable removing) and simply dance for 60 seconds without thinking about dancing. Use your legs, hands, arms, head, butt, nose, and fingers. Just let your body move and dance. If you try this four or five times with an open mind and heart, you'll be amazed at how loose you become. Let go of all those tapes in your head demanding that you grow up and act your age! Whose voice is that, anyway? Just let go and have fun. Like being a kid again, huh? What was that like? How do you feel? Would you do this crazy dance again?

2. **Seeing an old friend**

   If you have access to a videotape recorder, record one of your speech practice sessions. Tape at least five minutes of one practice. Then replay the video *without sound*. It's important that you don't have sound. Without the sound, your body will "talk" to you. Look at what your body says. Watch all of you—the face, gestures, body, arms, legs, fingers, and eyes. What does this body tell you? How does this body move? Is this body happy? Sad? Stiff? Loose? What's going on with this body? Does it make a difference when you add sound? How does it feel when you black out the video portion and simply listen to your voice? What did you learn about yourself?

3. **The body in other cultures**

   Ask an individual from a different cultural background what his or her people's attitudes and behaviors are in regards to their bodies. Do they value and attempt to demonstrate expressive gestures when speaking? How do they feel about eye contact? Is it encouraged or discouraged? Is a conversational tone of voice appropriate for public speaking or is a more formal style valued? What do they see as unusual or inappropriate nonverbal communication behavior?

Class Activities

1. **Group practice: Expanding your delivery**

   Divide the class into groups of five or six students. Each student will be given an opportunity to practice a speech (that he or she has already outlined) using the silent hula, catching rain, and singing exercises presented in this chapter. For 30 seconds, each student will stand in front of the group and perform the silent hula as he or she presents (nonverbally) the introduction to a speech. After the entire group has completed the silent hula, each student will practice the catching rain technique for 60 seconds as he or she delivers the first point of their speech to the group. And finally, each group member will sing 60 seconds of his or her second point. No fair talking! Only singing will count. What was this like to experiment with and expand your delivery skills? Be prepared to share your reactions to this group activity in class.

2. **Getting rid of the "ahs" and "ums"**

"Ahs," "ums," and all other verbal pauses are really apologies for silence in this culture. It's as if we're embarrassed to have any silences in our speech. We needed to apologize for not having something to say immediately, so we fill in the silence with "ahs" and "ums." Verbal pauses are distracting when they dominate our speech patterns. If you have trouble with them, try this exercise with a friend. Stand up in front of her, and deliver your practice speech. When she notices you saying a verbal pause ("ah" or "um" or anything else) she simply smiles and raises her hand briefly. This signals to you that you have done it again—given an apology for silence. She doesn't have to verbally interrupt you. She only raises her hand. This is also her signal to you that it's okay to pause and think about what you're going to say. When you first try this, you'll find that your partner's hand will be going up quite a bit. But after a while, if you permit yourself to pause before you speak, her hand will be raised less and less. Share your reactions to this activity in class.

3. **Out-of-class speaker evaluation**

Observe an out-of-class speaker and evaluate his or her effectiveness using the speaker evaluation form in this chapter, one provided by your instructor, or one you designed for this assignment. Observe a speaker in a formal speaking situation, such as a minister, politician, author, after-dinner speaker, or special-occasion lecturer. Take notes as the speaker is talking, using your evaluation form as a guide. Write a report discussing the strengths and weaknesses of the speaker. Share your observations and insights with the class.

NOTE

1. Albert Mehrabian, "Inference of Attitudes from Nonverbal Communication in Two Channels," *Journal of Consulting Psychology,* 31 (1967).

8

INFORMING YOUR AUDIENCE
Teaching Others

During the day, Building 7 at Campbell High School serves as the class-room for nearly 110 boys and girls in five classes of Auto Mechanics and Body Repair. Each period, this large, airplane hangar of a room echoes with the sounds of banging and clanging, buzzing and pounding. The students enroll in auto shop to learn the basic skills for a future trade or, more likely, because they didn't enjoy the math and science classes during their first two years of high school. Regardless of their motives, they all rush through the tall sliding metal doors of Building 7 when the bell sounds, laughing and shoving as they scurry to their next class.

Six nights of the week, Building 7 lies dark, empty, and silent until 7:20 the next morning, when the auto shop teacher unlocks the tall, silver sliding metal doors and flicks on the fluorescent lights, signaling the start of another noisy day in auto shop.

But tonight, Building 7 is transformed into a place of empowerment. A place where 11 women are learning to master their own lives in a small way and overcome some fears. These women are standing around the engine compartment of a 1987 Toyota Corolla, as Mr. Carl shows them how to change the oil and filter.

In a few moments, each woman will return to her car and begin the process of changing her own oil and filter as Mr. Carl walks among the students, answering their questions, correcting their mistakes, and con-gratulating their successes.

For the past six years, Mr. Carl has been teaching the Adult Education course entitled "Easy Car Maintenance for Women," and nearly 200 women have learned to maintain their own cars thanks to his instruc-tion. The students grow to love this quiet, slow-talking, 74-year-old retired auto mechanic, who wears a white shirt and red bowtie under his dark blue, Montgomery Ward coveralls. They love the way he asks them about their kids during the eight o'clock break, the way he pats them on the shoulder when they finish changing their oil, and the cookies he bakes himself for the one-night-a-week course. They grow to love this old man whose hands are scarred from years of working with tools, yet whose eyes sparkle in the fluorescent light.

Mr. Carl was once asked why he worked as a part-time teacher at an age when others are content to sit in retirement. "For over 50 years I've worked as an auto mechanic," he replied, "and nearly all that time was spent in silence under car hoods. When I retired eight years ago, I felt the need to pass on my trade to others. I felt this strong desire to share my knowledge and skills with people before I died."

Through Mr. Carl's teaching, 200 women in and around the city of Campbell won't have to pay to have their oil and filter changed, because they now possess the skill and knowledge to do it themselves. More importantly, these women can share their knowledge and skills with others, and thus, pass on the legacy of Mr. Carl.

Like Mr. Carl, your role as a public speaker will often be that of a teacher. You may not see yourself as a teacher, like Mr. Carl, yet one of the primary responsibilities of a public speaker is to inform the audience. To impart knowledge. To show the audience new skills. To share information that is important, interesting, and maybe even life changing. With your words alone, you may literally change the lives of the audience by sharing information that is truly meaningful and enlarging.

Now, you will most likely not be giving speeches every day of your life, but the ever-increasing emphasis on information in our world will demand greater skills in your ability to send and receive information. Although some of this information will be delivered in written form, much of it will be orally transmitted.

How do you inform others? How do you give directions, describe a scene, demonstrate a process, explain a concept, define a word, or tell a story? These areas of communication involve sharing information with others. Those who can inform others effectively will experience greater success in their professional and personal lives than those who cannot. Although this chapter will focus on your public speaking skills, you will find its application useful in your daily interactions with others as well.

GOALS OF INFORMATIVE SPEAKING

As an informative speaker, you face quite a challenge speaking before any audience. Some audiences are more receptive than others; and yet, each member of your audience needs to have his or her interest aroused, understand what you are saying, and remember the information after you've finished speaking. These are the three primary goals of any informative talk: to stimulate interest, increase understanding, and assist retention.

Stimulate Audience Interest

Your first goal of informative speaking is to arouse the interest of your audience. Without the successful completion of this first goal, the other two goals will not be accomplished. The old saying "There are no uninteresting topics, just uninterested listeners" affirms the need for you to get your audience aroused.

An experienced instructor once advised a first-year teacher, "Forget all that stuff they taught you in graduate school. The first requirement of a good teacher is to keep the students awake. Everything else is secondary." The same holds true for public speaking. If your audience's interest is not adequately stimulated, the prospects for a successful speech are dim indeed.

If you present your information in ways that make it *relevant* or personally useful to your audience, you are more inclined to arouse and maintain their interest. This is where audience analysis really pays off. Study your audience's interests, knowledge, attitudes, and demographics before selecting the materials you will present and how you will adapt that material to your specific audience.

Make the information relevant to where they are, not where you are. Bring your information close to where the audience lives. Drop it right in their laps. Present your material in ways that will make your audience realize, "I didn't know it affected me in that way." If you're talking about the importance of healthy eating habits to a group of young college students, make it relevant to them by describing how the accumulated effects of eating processed and fried foods will make life miserable for them in the future. Explain how increased risks of cancer, heart disease, diabetes, and other diseases multiply when their diet is saturated with these foods. Ask them how they will feel when their bodies fail and they can't do the things they take for granted today. Ask them if that's the future that they want to have. Make your topic hit home for your audience. Make it relevant.

If your speech information is *new,* the audience is more apt to pay attention. This principle of newness is seen in the marketing of products on your grocery store shelves. The words "new" and "improved" are splashed across the labels of hundreds of products annually. It seems that marketing research discovered that if the consumer perceived that a product was "new," he would be more likely to buy it. For your speaking purposes, new information will not be difficult to find. So use new information when it's appropriate.

There are some topics that are well-worn subjects for discussion, such as weight loss, exercise, or smoking. These topics are often met with disinterest by many. But you could present one of those topics in a different light or from a slightly different angle to give it freshness. For example, a talk on computers could be presented so that the audience could see their application for possible dating or mate selection, employment assistance, or vacation rental help, rather than the usual spread-sheet and word-processing functions.

Information is more likely to stimulate audience interest when it is *startling*. When we are startled, we are emotionally shaken, and all of our attention is focused on dealing with the source of that surprise. To hear a warning from the speaker that skin cancer is on the upswing in America may arouse our interest. But to hear that some scientists predict that in 20 years, one out of every three adults will experience some form of skin cancer by the time he or she reaches middle age will have a startling impact on the audience.

Increase Audience Understanding

The second goal of informative speaking is to present the information in a way that will be understood by your audience. Simple language, clear organization, examples, and visualization are four ways you can help your audience understand what you are saying.

The first way you can increase understanding is to use *simple language* when you speak to an audience. Aristotle once advised, "Think as wise men think, but speak as the common people speak." Some years ago, one of the foremost authorities on American economics taught at the University of California at Berkeley. She had authored several books on economics and had testified before Congress on numerous occasions, discussing our nation's economic woes. This expert was intelligent, gifted, and accomplished. But when she spoke in her Economics 2 course, the majority of her students didn't understand half the words she used. The students left her lectures feeling confused, frustrated, and often cheated. Here she is, "Ms. Economics Expert," and she couldn't speak in a style they could understand. What a waste of time! Lincoln cautioned, "We should speak so the least intelligent in the room can understand our words, then everyone will understand."

A speech that is *clearly organized* will help your audience understand what you have to say. The newspaper-writing adage to "tell them what you're going to tell them, tell them, and then, tell them what you told them" works with public speaking audiences as well. Remember the preview of main points, main-point transitions, and the summary of main points?

We need to remember that speaking is different from reading. The reader can *see* the various headings and subheadings, see the paragraph structure on the printed page. But the listener cannot. He must rely on *hearing* the words of the speaker. Make your speech easy to understand by previewing the points, stating clear transitions, and reviewing the points.

The third way you can increase understanding is to use *examples* in the development of your speech. Providing examples is one of the most concrete ways of helping your audience understand the ideas, concepts, and feelings you are trying to communicate. Every main point or concept you are trying to share with your audience should be accompanied by an example, be it brief or detailed. Stories are useful in developing a point you are trying to have the audience understand. The advantage of telling stories is they have a definite beginning, middle, and ending, and they usually captivate the audience's attention more effectively than shorter forms of examples. Another advantage is that a story is far easier to master and share with an audience than a list of statistics and facts. And the audience will most likely remember a well-told story long after the statistics and quotations have been forgotten.

The fourth way you can help your audience understand what your speech is about is to have them *visualize*. Visual aids are worth the effort they require because the dividends they pay in helping your audience see and understand what you're discussing are great. You can also have your audience visualize without the use of physical props. Many things you talk about cannot be adequately described on paper, such as the distance to the nearest star, the weight of the earth, or the speed of light. These concepts can be visualized by the audience when you have them "see" them in terms of something more familiar. For example, a speaker may describe the information storage capacity of one microchip as equal to the amount of information that could be stored in 100 full-size books!

Assist Audience Retention

The third goal of informative speaking is to help your audience remember what you have said. Now don't get your hopes too high. Studies in listening and retention clearly suggest that we don't remember all that much of what we hear. Immediately after we listen to a lecture, we generally retain only 50 percent of the material presented. Within two weeks we can remember only 25 percent of what was said.[1] There is some recent research that would lead us to believe that the actual figures are much lower.

What can you do to help the audience remember what you said? Much of it is out of your hands, I'm afraid to say. *Retention* is determined to a large extent by the listener's motivation, interests, training, psychological state, physical health, life circumstance, stress level, work schedule, interpersonal conflicts, and numerous other competing demands.

But there are still some specific things you can do to increase the probability that the audience will retain some of the information. The use of repetition, association, acronyms, one-sentence sayings, and handouts helps your audience remember your talk.

Repetition is a useful tool in your attempts to help your audience remember what you said. You can use it to repeat a thought. "This is so important, let me repeat that idea for you one more time," or "I need to say it again." Your preview and summary of main points in the introduction and conclusion of your speech are a form of repetition. You can also repeat the main point you are completing before going on to your next point by saying, "Now that we've looked at America in the 1970s, we can move on to our second point, and that's how America looked in the 1980s."

The use of *association* is a powerful tool for helping people retain information. Its purpose is for the listener to associate one thing with another. Usually, you have a listener associate a known quantity with an unknown quantity. For example, suppose you are trying to describe the workings of a jet engine to an audience of sixth graders. You might want to say the jet engine pushes out air and forces the plane forward, just as a balloon is thrust forward when you blow it up and let it go. Hopefully, the kids can make the association between the engine and the balloon. If you can use association in your speech, your audience will more likely remember your talk.

An *acronym* is something you're probably not too familiar with. It's a word formed from the initial letters of groups of words in a set phrase. The acronym is a very creative and effective technique when you want your audience to remember the main points of your speech. For example, if you presented a speech on acceptance skills in communication, you could use the acronym "MOM" to help the audience remember the three main points, which are "Mingle, Openness, and Mirroring." Acronyms are a simple way of having your audience retain the main points of your speeches. Here's another example.

Recently a young woman gave a talk on three aspects of communication. They were: (1) talk is cheap, watch behavior; (2) attitude is more important than aptitude; and (3) perception is communication. To help the audience remember her three points, she had them recite the word "TAP," which represented the first letters of the first words of each principle: "T" for "Talk," "A" for "Attitude," and "P" for "Perception." After she gave the speech and was getting into her car in the parking lot of the auditorium, a young man came up to her, smiled, and said "TAP, talk, attitude, and perception. I remembered your speech." He smiled and walked on. He didn't say anything else, simply that, and kept walking. But he had remembered the main points of her talk. Use a simple acronym, and your listeners will remember your speech too.

A fourth method for getting your audience to remember your talk is the use of a *one-sentence saying* that summarizes the theme or central idea of your speech. The sentence can be one you construct yourself, a quotation, a proverb, a verse from a poem, a title from a movie or book, or anything else that is no longer than a sentence and easy to remember. If you use the one-sentence technique, state the sentence in the introduction, the transitions to each main point, and the conclusion.

For example, a speaker gave a speech entitled "Premarital Sex and You" to high school students at a summer retreat. In the speech, the young man addressed the social, psychological, and physical wounds that premarital sex could inflict on the lives of those high school students. The one sentence the speaker used as the theme for the talk was simply "Going to bed can cost you plenty." He must have used that sentence 10 times in the speech. "Going to bed can cost you plenty." Your one-sentence saying can have a powerful impact on the audience's retention of your message. Keep your message simple, and keep your audience focused so they'll remember.

The final thing you can do to help your audience remember your speech is to prepare a *one-page handout* highlighting the important points of your talk. You can simply outline the key points and include suggested readings. Leave some space between your key ideas on the handout so the listener can jot down notes or things to remember. If you invest the extra time and energy these handouts require, the payoff can be significant, because the listeners have something in their hot little hands to help them remember your speech.

DESIGNS FOR INFORMATIVE SPEAKING

There are three basic designs or strategies for constructing an informative speech that we'll be examining next: exposition, description, and narration. Most informative speeches use a combination of two or more of these designs in their construction.

Exposition

The first approach to informative speaking is exposition. *Exposition* means to expose or explain. Therefore, the main goal of exposition is to inform your audience. Exposition is used to explain a process, concept, or idea to others. You've used this form of informative speaking before when you've given directions to your home, told a story, described a restaurant, or defined a word. There are three forms of exposition: definition, demonstration, and analysis.

The first form of exposition is *definition*. If you want to give your audience a clear idea of what you're talking about, they will have to understand the words and concepts presented in your talk. It's important that you define words or concepts that may be unfamiliar, vague, or abstract to your listeners. When you define a word or concept, use simple language. If it's possible, use your own words to define the term. Try to avoid dictionary or technical definitions, because they tend to sound stiff and lifeless to the listener. The definition is the fundamental building block of all informative speaking. Without an understanding of your words and concepts, your audience will be lost in your speech. There are three ways that you can make your definitions clear to your audience: example, comparison, and etymology.

When you define a word by *example*, you use examples to clarify the word or concept. An example is something that is used to illustrate a point. To define by example is especially helpful when you are trying to clarify a vague or abstract word. When using examples, you can use the actual object, such as showing a fighting saber when talking about samurai swords. Or you can give a verbal example of brotherly love as you define a certain aspect of the abstract term "love."

Comparison can also be used to define a word or concept, by comparing the word to something that is known to the audience. If you can relate a new word or concept to something that is already understood by the audience, you will be more successful in getting your message across. A speaker trying to define the concept of balancing on a surfboard might compare it to walking on a railroad track or riding a skateboard.

The third form of definition uses etymology. Often it is useful to trace the origin and development of a word in your attempts to give clarity. This is called *etymology*—the study of the origin and development of words. A speaker once traced the word "sarcasm" to its original Greek term *sarkasmos,* which meant "to rend or rip flesh." The original Greek definition gave her audience a much more descriptive picture of her term.

When attempting to inform your audience about a process, demonstration, the second form of exposition, works well. *Demonstration* enables you to actually show the audience how something works or how something is made. The use of demonstration can also involve the participation of your audience. If the subject of your speech is emergency water safety techniques, and you are demonstrating the technique used for relaxing a muscle cramp in your leg, you could have the audience actually rub their own legs to get a feel for the technique, or you could demonstrate it yourself.

A demonstration speech would be appropriate if you were going to speak on such topics as making sushi, repairing a lamp, cutting hair, showing how a vacuum cleaner works, checking for skin cancer, or binding a book. Some of these topics would lend themselves to audience participation, whereas others would not. Consider the choice carefully before you invite audience participation.

Review the suggestions on visual-aid usage discussed earlier if you will be using demonstration in your speech. If you are going to demonstrate a process or show how something works for your audience, here are some additional suggestions for you to consider when constructing and delivering your talk.

Cluster the steps of your demonstration into a maximum of three or four main points. Even the simplest of processes requires a multitude of ministeps for its completion. Your goal is to cluster these ministeps into three or four major clusters or categories. For instance, the seemingly simple process of tossing a salad contains a number of steps that would confuse an audience if you were to present each one as a main point. Instead, cluster these many steps into three main points, such as "Gather the materials, prepare the ingredients, and toss the salad." Other cluster designs, such as "Plan, Do, Finish," and "Gather Materials, Do the Process, and Clean Up," are useful when trying to put your process into some recognizable form. Clustering your steps provides clarity of organization for your audience and ease of handling for you.

Another way you can help your audience understand and remember your demonstration is to *preview and review main points in the introduction and conclusion* of your speech. Remember that you need to lead your audience by the hand and clearly orient and review the process. If you want to get really organized and impressive, number the steps in your preview and summary of main points, so it sounds like, "The first step is to gather the materials, the second step is to mix the ingredients, and the third and final step is to bake the cake."

The final suggestion for demonstrating a process is to include *dead-time talk*. When a speaker is actually demonstrating the slicing of the vegetables, the carving of the wood, or the mixing of the ingredients, there is a tendency on the part of the speaker to focus on the process and not talk. In other words, the audience is watching the process, and the speaker is not saying a word. That's okay if the silence lasts a few seconds, but 20 or 30 seconds of silence could make your audience feel uncomfortable. This dead time should be filled with some discussion. When you are demonstrating a process in a speech and you have 20 or 30 seconds of possible dead time, share a brief anecdote about the first time you ever did the process or a humorous incident that happened to you when you were doing this process. This dead-time talk not only fills the silence, it adds color and substance to your talk.

The third form of exposition is analysis. *Analysis* is the breaking down of an idea, concept, or event into its various parts to get a clearer picture of how something operates or functions. The review of a play or movie, the structure of the federal government, an evaluation of the strengths and weaknesses of a proposal, and the development of the space program are topics that could utilize analysis in their presentation.

When presenting to an audience topics that could possibly be difficult to understand—such as a budget report, an organizational flowchart, or a newly implemented time management program—dividing the concept into its component parts for closer examination is always beneficial.

Description

The second approach to informative speaking is description. *Description* makes use of sensory information to verbally paint a clear picture of what you're talking about without the use of visual aids. The categories of description that you can use are size, shape, weight, color, composition, and age.

Size can be described in terms such as "big" or "small," "large" or "tiny," but these terms are subjective and relative. They can mean different things to different listeners. It's much better to be specific when describing size to your audience. A speaker can describe a cut on the arm as a "large cut," but that description does not paint the same picture as another description with specific dimensions. A cut that is described as "eight inches in length, half an inch wide, and two inches deep" paints a picture that would make even the sturdiest of listeners squirm in their seats.

Shape can be described in geometric forms, such as square, triangular, round, spherical, and rectangular. "His face was square with a cone nose," "The racetrack is oblong," and "Her house looked like a rectangular box" are examples of using shape to describe objects.

The *weight* of an object, like its size, can be described in a subjective and relative fashion, such as "light," "heavy," "featherweight," or "hefty." A more descriptive way to describe an object's weight is to report in ounces, pounds, and tons. Instead of saying that "the man was heavy," you could describe the man as "weighing 500 pounds, or one-quarter of a ton."

Color is the fourth category of description you can use when painting a mental picture of the object you are describing. The obvious labels of black and white, red and green help give the audience a clearer picture of what you're communicating. It's useful to link the color to a common object that is familiar to the audience's experience, such as "red as a cherry," "blue as the ocean," or "black as a moonless night."

The *composition* of an object provides further detail to the picture you are painting. Composition refers to the makeup or construction of an object. "His legs looked like plucked chicken skin," "The lake was as smooth as glass," and "His hair was matted down like oiled feathers" are examples of composition.

A final category of description is *age*. The usual descriptors of "new" and "old" are helpful in painting a picture of an object. But once again, more specific descriptions of age, such as months, years, and centuries, provide more vividness. To describe the sofa as "being in our family for over 50 years" gives us a better appreciation for its age than to simply describe it as "an old sofa."

Narration

The third form of informative speaking is *narration*. Storytelling is the oldest form of passing information from one generation to another. Before the written word, myths of the creation, stories explaining life's mysteries, and rituals that bound tribes and cultures together were passed on in the form of stories. Century after century, these stories were handed down through the generations.

In public speaking, storytelling or narration can be used as a powerful means of clarifying an idea or concept for your audience. Equally important is the ability of a story to stick in the listener's memory long after the story has been told. When you use narration in your speech to describe an important concept or idea, you might consider these suggestions:

Your story should illustrate your point. Don't include a story in your speech just because it's your favorite. Your story must illustrate, demonstrate, or clarify a point you are trying to make with your audience.

Know your story. You should be so familiar with your story that you could tell it without the use of notes. Know the correct pronunciation of all the words, names, and places contained in the story. You should know your story so well that you become the story.

Become the various characters. When reciting dialogue, use the voices of the various characters in your story. This may feel awkward at first, but it will present a better story to your listeners if you sound like the "old woman," the "frightened boy," or the "mean old king." Your nonverbal behavior can also be a way of taking on the personality of the various characters. Use the posture, walk, gestures, and facial expressions of the different characters so your audience can also "see" the story you are telling.

Time your story during your practice sessions. It often takes longer to tell a story than you would expect. You get caught up in the characterization, the detail, and the emotions of the story, and before you know it, your speaking time is up. Time your story when you practice your speech. You may have to cut a little here and there to get the story to conform to the time requirements.

LANGUAGE USE FOR INFORMATIVE SPEAKING

Before we outline the basic types of informative speeches, we need to mention some additional recommendations for the effective use of language in your presentations. The message sent isn't always the message received, and the following suggestions will help you in your attempts to communicate clearly with your audience in all types of public speaking.

Simple Language

Many beginning speakers feel the need to impress an audience with highly elaborate, ornate, or complex language. So instead of saying, "The group members were residents of Spain," a speaker might state, "The group members were denizens of Spain." "Denizens" sounds fine, but who knows what it means? The speaker, in her attempt to sound impressive, increases her chances of losing her audience. Use language that is simple and readily understood by your audience. Avoid using technical language or jargon that is foreign or unfamiliar to your audience. If you must use specialized vocabulary, define the words clearly and simply so your audience can understand what you mean. Finally, when using acronyms, make certain that you explain what each letter represents. For instance, "AA stands for Alcoholics Anonymous," or "CPR stands for cardiopulmonary resuscitation." You might assume your audience knows what the letters stand for, but if you're wrong, you've just lost more of your listeners along the way.

Specific Language

Avoid using vague or abstract language in your speeches. Overused words and clichés should also be avoided. If you use language that is vague or overused, the audience isn't challenged, and they may begin to drift off to other things in the room besides you. You don't want that. So use words that are as specific and concrete as possible. Instead of saying, "The woman planted some flowers in her yard," you might want to use more specific words by stating, "The woman planted purple tulips, yellow roses, and red geraniums in her yard." Do you notice the difference? Which scene do you see more vividly? Remember to use specific words in your language.

Active Language

Use strong, active verbs in your speeches. Avoid using weak verbs such as "is," "was," "will be," and "are." Instead of saying, "It is my feeling that...," you can more forcefully announce, "I feel...." Which of the following two statements sounds more assertive: "This matter needs *to be* brought before the board of directors" or "This matter *demands* the attention of the board of directors"? Your choice of verbs will make a critical difference in the movement, urgency, and flow of your speeches. Will your language put the audience to sleep or take them for a roller-coaster ride?

Personal Language

Language that is personal in nature will have a greater impact in reaching your audience than more formal or distant language. The use of personal pronouns such as "I," "you," "us," and "we" will help to bring you closer to your audience. Their use can make the audience feel that you are interested in them and understand their concerns and desires. Notice the difference between these two sentences: "Americans need to get a physical exam once every two years" and "You need to get a physical exam once every two years." The first sentence is directed to 230 million people. The second sentence is delivered to only one person. Language that is personal will bridge that gap between you and your listeners.

Guiding Language

Talking about bridges.... Another way you can use language more effectively in helping your audiences understand and remember your speech is to use language that guides them in, around, and through your presentation. Transitions are the best devices the speaker can utilize in guiding and directing the listener. External transitions are complete sentences used to signal movement from one major part of the speech to another. Between the main points of your speech, external transitions are essential in directing the listener from one point to another. "Now that I've discussed the history of the radio, let's move to my second point, and that's the innovations after World War II." This transition even recapped the previous main point ("Now that I've discussed...") before signaling movement into the second point of the talk. Internal transitions are those words and phrases that signal movement between the smaller parts of a sentence or main point.

Internal transitions such as *and, also, but, however, although, because, on the other hand, for example, therefore,* and *finally* all signal relationships between the smaller parts of sentences or main points. Use internal transitions to keep your thoughts connected to one another, and your listeners connected to your speech. Transitions are the verbal bridges that show the relationships between your points and thoughts, and they keep you linked to your audience.

Positive Language

Ultimately, you want to have a positive effect on your audience. Not only do you want them to understand and remember your message, you want them to perceive you as a credible speaker. Someone they can trust and respect. You may even want them to like you. We're only human. In addition to the obvious recommendations of using appropriate language (no swearing or vulgarity) and avoiding emotionally loaded words or terms (don't refer to Texans as "rednecks" while addressing the Texas Republican Convention), you should be complimentary to your listeners whenever you can. Begin your talk by thanking the audience for the invitation to address them. Research the audience or group so you can mention in your speech one or two things they've accomplished recently. And end with a final appeal that is in accordance with the group's goals and objectives.

Above all, you want to have an enlarging impact on your listeners. They should feel that their time with you was well spent, and your positive language and attitude will help to guarantee this goal.

TYPES OF INFORMATIVE SPEECHES

Now that we've examined the goals and designs for informative speaking, let's turn our attention finally to the various types of informative speeches. The three primary informative-speech designs are: expository, descriptive, and narrative. Sample main-point structures for each of the various types of speeches to inform follow.

Expository Speeches

Definition Speech
Specific Purpose: To define three aspects of success.

    I. The first aspect is personal fulfillment.
   II. The second aspect is intellectual stimulation.
  III. The third aspect is social contribution.

Demonstration Speech
Specific Purpose: To demonstrate the three steps required in baking cookies.

    I. The first step is to gather your materials.
   II. The second step is to mix the ingredients.
  III. The third step is to bake the cookies.

Analysis Speech
Specific Purpose: To describe the three branches of the federal government.

I. The first branch of the federal government is the legislative branch.
II. The second branch of the federal government is the judicial branch.
III. The third branch of the federal government is the executive branch.

Descriptive Speeches

Describing a Person
Specific Purpose: To describe three characteristics of George Washington.

I. The first characteristic of Washington is that he was very intelligent.
II. The second characteristic of Washington is that he possessed a brilliant military mind.
III. The third characteristic of Washington is that he was a persuasive speaker.

Describing a Place
Specific Purpose: To describe three Lake Tahoe attractions.

I. The first attraction is Lake Tahoe's beautiful lake.
II. The second attraction is Lake Tahoe's campgrounds.
III. The third attraction is Lake Tahoe's hiking trails.

Describing an Event
Specific Purpose: To explain the Denver Broncos' Super Bowl journey.

I. The first stage was the preseason training.
II. The second stage was the regular season.
III. The third stage was the Super Bowl playoff postseason.

Narrative Speeches

Personal-Experience Narrative
Specific Purpose: To relate my aircrash adventure in Montana.

I. I was flying to Montana in a Piper Cub airplane.
II. Inclement weather forced the plane to crash in the foothills of eastern Montana.
III. I survived six days before being rescued by forest rangers.

Historical Narrative
Specific Purpose: To explain the bombing of Pearl Harbor.

    I. The Japanese planned the attack for two years.
   II. The surprise attack was devastating in terms of loss of lives.
  III. The attack forced the United States into World War II.

ANSWERING QUESTIONS FROM THE AUDIENCE

After you have concluded a speech, you may want to give your audience the opportunity to ask questions. The question-and-answer period is one of the areas you will need to be skilled in if you are to be a capable speaker. Here are some suggestions that will help you:

1. Assume your audience will ask questions.
2. Ask for audience questions cheerfully and with a smile.
3. Restate the question to the entire audience ("The question is…"). This gives you time to think, lets the audience know the question, and keeps the audience's attention on you.
4. Answer the question succinctly. A common mistake is to say too much and give a second speech. Don't bore the rest of the audience.
5. Stimulate the audience (if no response) by using any of the following statements:

    "A question that is often asked is…"
    "Have you ever considered…?"
    "One thing I didn't have time to address was…"

Sample Informative Speech Outline

The Three-Step Listening Process

Specific Purpose: To inform the audience on the three-step listening process.

Introduction

Has a loved one ever said to you, "You don't understand me"? Have you ever been told, "You're not really hearing what I'm saying"? And has anyone complained, "You're not interested in what I'm telling you"? Well, listening is a vital component of communication with loved ones, and we can all improve our listening skills. Today, I want to share with you a three-step process for effective listening. First, you need to provide a nonevaluative listening atmosphere. Second, you need to paraphrase what the speaker is saying. And third, you need to negotiate meaning with the speaker.

Continued

Continued

Body

I. *The first step in listening is to provide a nonevaluative listening atmosphere.*
   A. Be physically receptive when you are listening.
      1. Stephen Covey, in his book *The 7 Habits of Highly Effective Families* states, "You need to be physically attentive as you listen to others."
      2. Maintain eye contact with the speaker.
      3. Nod occasionally to acknowledge the speaker.
   B. Listen without verbal interruption as the speaker talks.
      1. Avoid the usual tendency to evaluate or judge.
      2. Avoid the usual tendency to problem-solve or rescue.
      3. Share story of listening to friend without interrupting.

II. *The second step in listening is to paraphrase what the speaker has shared.*
   A. Ron Adler and Neil Towne, in their book *Looking Out, Looking In* suggest that "Questioning is often the most valuable tool for increasing understanding."
   B. Paraphrase the speaker's statement with reflecting questions.
      1. "Are you saying…?"
      2. "Do you mean…?"

III. *The third step is to negotiate meaning with the speaker.*
   A. If the speaker agrees with your paraphrase, state your own response or opinion.
   B. If the speaker disagrees with your paraphrase, paraphrase a second time.
      1. If the speaker agrees, state your own response or opinion.
      2. If the speaker disagrees, attempt to paraphrase again until the speaker agrees.
   C. Marriage and family counselor, Jack Seiquist, has said, "Effective communication requires negotiating meaning. This process is one of the most demanding, yet rewarding activities we engage in during our lives."
   D. Story about how I used this listening process with my father.

Conclusion

Today, I've shared with you the three-step process for effective listening. First, you need to provide a nonevaluative listening atmosphere. Second, you need to paraphrase what the speaker is saying. And third, you need to negotiate meaning with the speaker. It is my hope that you will try this three-step process the next time you find yourself in an important discussion.

Bibliography

Ron Adler and Neil Towne. *Looking Out / Looking In.* Fort Worth, Texas: Harcourt Brace Jovanovich, 1996.
Stephen Covey. *The 7 Habits of Highly Effective Families.* New York: Golden Books, 1997.
Jack Seiquist, MFCC. Interview on September 3, 1998, in San Jose, Calif.

COMMUNICATION ACTIVITIES

Personal Activities

1. **The best teacher**

   Who was the best teacher you have had in your life? What did he or she teach? What did this person teach you about yourself? What did you like or appreciate about this teacher? Can you identify any specific techniques or approaches in their informative speaking that you felt were especially effective in helping you learn? Can you identify any specific delivery characteristics that captivated and held your attention? Which of these delivery and informative-speaking techniques might you use in your own personal speaking? Have you ever written this teacher a thank-you note for their contribution to your learning?

2. **What do you teach others?**

   Although you may not realize it, you are always teaching those around you by your example. Little kids in the neighborhood, your family members, those at work, and your friends observe your actions over time. It's not really what you say that's important. It's what you do. What does your behavior say about you? Do you keep promises? Are you punctual? Are you enlarging? Do you listen without interrupting? Do you encourage? Can you keep a secret? Do you touch? Are you there when others need a friend? What does your behavior teach others about you?

3. **Teachers in other cultures**

   Ask an individual from a different cultural background about his or her culture's attitudes and behaviors toward teachers. Are teachers valued? Are they respected? How are they paid? What are the primary teaching methods of instruction? How do students interact with their teachers? What classroom attitudes and behaviors are different from ours? How are they similar?

Class Activities

1. **Group discussion: Brainstorm informative speech topics**

   Divide the class into groups of five or six students. Each group is to brainstorm a minimum of 30 possible topics for informative speaking. What topics are of interest to the group? Remember not to evaluate or judge any of the suggestions offered by the group members. After the group has completed its list, review the list and discuss which topics might be of interest to the entire class. Which topics might not be of interest? Why? Be prepared to share your group's list with the class.

2. **Explanation speech**

   Prepare, practice, and present a three-to-five-minute informative speech explaining a word, concept, theory, or idea. Develop each of your three main points with documented information and examples. Include any visual aids that might be helpful. Your speech should contain an introduction, body, and conclusion.

3. **Demonstration speech**

   Prepare, practice, and present a five-to-seven-minute demonstration speech showing how something is made or how something works. Use the cluster method of arranging the main points of your speech. Develop each of your main points with documented information and examples. Include any visual aids that might be helpful. Your speech should contain an introduction, body, and conclusion.

4. **Tribute speech**

   Prepare, practice, and present a five-to-seven minute tribute speech honoring someone who is important to your life. The purpose of this speech is to share three wonderful things about this individual with your audience. A tribute speech can be used to honor someone at a birthday, retirement party, anniversary, or eulogy. Your speech should contain an introduction, body, and conclusion.

5. **Informative speech**

   Prepare, practice, and present a five-to-seven minute speech on a topic that would be of interest to your audience. Research this topic thoroughly after analyzing your audience. Develop each of your main points with documented information and examples. Include any visual aids that might be helpful. Your speech should contain an introduction, body, and conclusion.

6. **What it's like to... speech**

   Prepare, practice, and present a five-to-seven-minute speech describing what it's like to be or do something. For instance, what it's like to be the oldest child, divorced, a twin, a police officer, an Asian American, an artist, a mechanic, or to parachute from an airplane. Research this topic thoroughly after analyzing your audience. Develop each of your main points with documented information and examples. Include any visual aids that might be helpful. Your speech should contain an introduction, body, and conclusion.

NOTE

1. Ralph Nichols, *Are You Listening?* (New York: McGraw-Hill, 1957).

9

PERSUADING YOUR AUDIENCE
Changing Others

Chio walked slowly to the podium for the final time. This public speaking class had proved to be the most challenging, yet most rewarding class she had ever taken. During the semester, Chio's five previous speeches had given her the skills and experience to approach this final speech with confidence.

As Chio reached the front of the classroom, she remembered the first time she had ever stood behind this podium just 12 weeks ago. She was frightened, disoriented, unable to look away from her notes even once. But since then, she had gradually developed her speaking skills and discovered a confidence that slowly filled her mind and heart with a quiet strength she had never felt before. This confidence had enabled Chio to successfully run for vice president of the Asian Club on campus. And it was as the newly elected Asian Club vice president that she would speak to her class for the final time.

During the next seven minutes, Chio would persuade more than a third of the students in class to actually attend the Open House BBQ hosted by the Asian Club. The BBQ was intended to get students of all races together for fun and conversation. The goal was to build bridges and not walls between students on campus.

She began her speech by asking how many students were interested in attending the BBQ. Only two of the 30 students raised their hands. By the end of her seven-minute persuasive speech, however, more than half the class raised their hands as Chio ended her talk with that same question. A few weeks later, 12 of her public speaking classmates shared in the delicious food, friendly conversations, and newly discovered friendships at the Asian Club picnic. In her speech, Chio had initiated the process of getting students together who would not normally socialize with one another. Because of her words during those seven minutes, Chio had convinced 10 people to change their thinking and experience something new. Because of her speech, Chio had built a bridge and not a wall between people of different backgrounds.

We are bombarded daily by persuasive appeals to purchase this product, contribute to that charity, or subscribe to this belief. We, in turn, try to convince someone to baby-sit our kids, ask the boss for a raise, or request the neighbor to turn down his stereo. Daily, we must deal with hundreds of persuasive events, whether we are conscious of them or not. Your ability to convince others and motivate them to action will, to a large extent, determine the quality and destiny of your life and that of those around you.

BASICS OF PERSUASION

Persuasion is the process of trying to get others to change their beliefs or behavior. Unlike informative speaking, where the goal is the sharing of information, persuasion is aimed at going a step further—changing others. This process of changing, and not simply sharing, is the focus of this chapter.

Three Purposes of Persuasion

In persuasive speaking, there are three different purposes we can attempt to achieve with an audience, although most persuasive appeals utilize a combination of all three. The persuasive purposes are to reinforce an already held belief, change a belief, and motivate to action.

The first persuasive purpose is to *reinforce an already held belief.* It is the goal of our persuasive appeals if we're speaking on such topics as "Everyone Should Vote" or "The Cure for AIDS Must Be Found." These are beliefs that are held by the majority of any group, and your speech will be directed to reinforcing or strengthening that belief.

A second persuasive purpose is to *change an audience belief.* This would be your goal if you were speaking on such topics as "We Should Ban Air-Conditioning in Cars" or "Citizens Should Be Allowed to Burn the American Flag." These beliefs are not held by the majority of your audience, and your goal in these instances would be to change their beliefs.

The final persuasive purpose is to *motivate to action.* This would be your goal if you were speaking on such topics as "Contribute Money to the Red Cross" or "Attend This Evening's City Council Meeting." The primary purpose in speeches like these is to get the audience members to actually do something.

Whether your goal is to reinforce a belief, change a belief, or motivate the audience to action, it should be clearly indicated in your proposition.

The Proposition

In persuasive speaking, the specific purpose or goal statement is called the proposition. The *proposition* is the desired effect that you want to have on your audience. What exactly is it that you want your audience to believe or do? Many persuasive attempts are doomed from the beginning because the speaker does not know exactly what she wants from the audience. A properly constructed proposition can ensure this clarity and specificity.

A proposition must be limited to one sentence. The intent and goal of the persuasive speech must be contained in that sentence. How do you want the audience to respond? If you want to strengthen an already held belief, you must phrase your proposition accordingly. For example, "To strengthen the audience's belief that everyone should take regular vacations" and "To reinforce the audience's belief that child abuse is a terrible crime" are two propositions that attempt to strengthen already held beliefs.

You can phrase your proposition to reflect a desire to change the audience's beliefs. For instance, "To convince the audience that we should not permit freedom of the press" and "To convince the audience that we should abolish home mortgage interest deductions on federal income tax" are two propositions that seek to change audience beliefs.

Finally, you can phrase your proposition to motivate your audience to action. Propositions such as "To persuade the audience to volunteer as a Big Brother or Big Sister" and "To motivate the audience to donate blood at the annual company blood drive" are seeking to get the listeners to do something.

A poorly phrased proposition will hinder your efforts to organize and deliver an effective persuasive appeal. Make certain that your proposition contains a clear and specific purpose and goal. When you are constructing your proposition, consider the following three suggestions:

Your proposition should meet an audience need. Your proposition will be more likely to succeed if you consider the needs of your particular audience, and design your proposition around those needs. If a person has a need for a computer, he will be more likely to receive a message on computers. If a person needs employment, he will be more likely to receive a message on employment opportunities or interviewing techniques. Your ability to analyze and consider audience needs will be valuable when deciding on your proposition.

Your proposition should be reasonable. To ask that each member of your audience donate $10,000 to a charitable organization or that they jog 10 miles a day is probably asking for more than most people are willing to give. Your proposition should be phrased with a reasonable goal in mind. It's the old "foot-in-the-door" technique; you begin by asking for something small and reasonable, then you build your argument or persuasive appeal to include more comprehensive objectives. Remember, in all things, moderation.

Your proposition should be simple. The more complex your proposition is, the more likely you are to confuse your audience. A multiple proposition can even have a counterproductive effect on your listeners. The proposition "To persuade the audience to rethink their current belief that milk is good for them, to believe that natural juices provide greater benefit to their overall physical and psychological health, and to invest in a one-week vacation at the Nirvana Health Food Resort" would not only be overwhelming in terms of evidence required, but it would place too much demand on the audience in terms of the sheer amount of persuasion asked for. A more manageable proposition might be "To convince the audience to drink natural juices" or "To persuade the audience to drink less milk." Keep it simple.

ARISTOTLE'S THREE PERSUASIVE PROOFS

Now that we've examined the persuasive purposes and the proposition, we can introduce the three persuasive proofs. More than 2,000 years ago, Aristotle divided all persuasive effort into three categories: ethos, logos, and pathos. *Ethos* is the ethical appeal or credibility of the speaker. *Logos* is the logical appeal. And *pathos* is the emotional appeal. We now examine how each of these three dimensions of persuasion can help you change and motivate others.

Ethos (Speaker Credibility)

Aristotle believed that the most important component of persuasion was the perceived credibility of the speaker or her ethical appeal. Is the speaker someone who can be trusted? Someone who has our best interests at heart? Someone who sounds like she knows what she's talking about? These and related questions shape our opinion of a speaker and will directly affect our response to her appeal. Ethos is the perceived credibility of the speaker. Ethos, or speaker credibility, consists of the speaker's competence, goodwill, and character.

The speaker's expertise or experience is called *competence*. We will generally listen to and believe a speaker we perceive as trained, knowledgeable, and experienced in a given subject or discipline area. A physician's knowledge, training, and experience all contribute to his overall competence in the field of medicine. The expertise of the knowledgeable professor makes him more believable than a professor who displays a poor command of the material. Your competence as a speaker can be enhanced by speaking on topics you have previous experience with or training in. You can also increase your perceived competence by providing your listeners with evidence and research from experts in the subject area you are discussing.

The second component of ethos is *goodwill*. We will generally believe people we like. Goodwill is the dimension of the speaker that deals with interpersonal warmth, friendliness, and enthusiasm. One of the reasons we like puppies is that they show friendliness and boundless energy toward us. If a speaker is cold, aloof, and condescending, our usual response is to reject that person. Some research suggests that the perceived goodwill of the speaker is the most important of the three elements of credibility.

How can you increase your sense of goodwill? First, show enthusiasm. Speakers who talk in a lifeless monotone, as if they were delivering a funeral eulogy, are generally received in similar fashion. Be enthusiastic in your nonverbal communication! Show some life! What goes around, comes around. Second, be friendly toward your audience. Use a speech style that is warm and friendly. Be personable. Smile. And third, use humor when appropriate. There's something about well-received humor that increases liking and attraction.

The third component of ethos is the speaker's character. *Character* is the overall makeup of a person. It's what the speaker is made of. Honesty, integrity, and trustworthiness are major elements of a person's character, and if the speaker seems to possess these traits, we are more likely to believe him than if he did not. An audience member must feel that she can trust and respect the speaker before she will be persuaded by that speaker.

What, then, can you do to be perceived as possessing an honest and trustworthy character? Here are some suggestions. First, dress appropriately. Your audience bases much of their evaluation of you by the manner in which you dress. Second, be truthful. Don't exaggerate points. Present your views fairly. Third, share your motives with the audience. Tell the audience why you are taking the position you are taking. Even if they disagree with you, they will appreciate your candidness. Finally, establish common ground with your audience. An audience will more likely feel better about you if you possess similar beliefs, values, attitudes, and experiences.

Let's close this section on ethical appeal with a word or two on the *ethical considerations of speaking*. As a public speaker, you have the ethical responsibility to put the interests of your audience before your own. You have the ethical responsibility to tell the truth. Treating your audience with respect, even if they do not agree with your position on a given issue, is a responsibility you have as a speaker as well. You also have the ethical responsibility to avoid doing anything that would hurt another person. Your words are extremely powerful. Be careful how you choose to use them, because it has been said that we will be held accountable for every word we utter. The law of Karma suggests that same principle.

Logos (Logical Appeal)

The second component of persuasion is logos. *Logos* is the logical appeal or the reasoning process presented by the speaker. *Reasoning* is the process of drawing conclusions from evidence. You will recall that evidence takes the form of either statistics or expert testimony. Let's examine the two basic forms of the reasoning process: deductive and inductive reasoning.

Deductive reasoning moves from a general rule or premise and applies it to a specific case. The flow is from the general to the specific. From big to small. An example of deductive reasoning would be:

1. Mary is a member of a church. (*premise*)
2. Therefore, Mary believes in God. (*specific conclusion*)

In most deductive reasoning, one of the premises is not stated. This is called an *enthymeme*. Let's look at the reasoning again and include the missing premise:

1. Members of a church believe in God. (*major premise*)
2. Mary is a member of a church. (*minor premise*)
3. Therefore, Mary believes in God. (*specific conclusion*)

When all three steps of the deductive reasoning process are stated, as in the example above, it is called a *syllogism*.

Let's see if you can fill in the part in the following syllogism:

1. All human beings are mortal.
2. Travis is a human being.
3. Therefore, _____.

(How was that? The answer is "Travis is mortal.")

Try to complete the missing information in this example:

1. All divorced people have been married.
2. _____.
3. Therefore, John has been married.

(Was this one easy for you? The answer to the minor premise is "John is divorced.")

Now, let's see how the syllogism can be used to test the deductive logic of a speech. Suppose that you want to convince your audience that automobile air-conditioning units are destroying our atmosphere. The syllogism would look something like this:

Major Premise: Freon gas destroys the earth's ozone layer.

Minor Premise: Most automobile air-conditioning units leak significant amounts of Freon into the atmosphere.

Conclusion: Therefore, automobile air-conditioning units are destroying the earth's ozone layer.

Now that you have constructed the syllogism, you will need to research and present evidence, both statistical and expert testimony, that will prove your major and minor premises to your audience. These can serve as the content for the first two points of your persuasive speech. If you succeed in getting your audience to agree with your major and minor premises, they should accept your conclusion. If used correctly, deductive logic can be an effective persuasive tool.

Whereas deductive reasoning moves from the general to the specific, *inductive reasoning* uses the opposite strategy. It examines specific examples or facts and then draws a general conclusion. Inductive reasoning moves from the small to the large, from the specific to the general.

Suppose you have owned three mutt dogs in your life, and each one of those mixed-breed dogs was friendly, well behaved, and healthy. From your experience and observation of those three specific dogs, you could arrive at the general conclusion that all mutt dogs make great pets. If you read statistics asserting that married couples who communicated regularly stayed married longer than couples who did not, you might conclude that regular communication is an important requirement for a long marriage. In both cases, you moved from specific observations or evidence to a general conclusion.

In the case in which your experience with three different mutt dogs led you to conclude that all mixed-breed dogs make great pets, you were using the inductive reasoning process. In other words, you said to yourself that what is true in some instances is true in all instances. This is a common form of inductive reasoning used by speakers.

In the second example of communication and marriage length, you were using *reasoning by statistics,* another form of inductive reasoning. Different pieces of statistical evidence, each pointing to the same conclusion, led to the belief that regular communication is important to a long-lasting marriage. Reasoning by statistics isn't readily accepted by all people, however. There are many who are suspicious of anything that resembles numerical data, and there is some basis for their skepticism. Statistics can be presented and interpreted in a variety of ways that can be misleading. Here are some suggestions for using statistics:

Document your statistics orally. If your audience is not familiar with the statistics you will be presenting, you need to document the evidence *before* you share it with your audience. You should cite the author, source, and date of the research. It can be cited as simply as:

> "Dr. Joe Smith, in his book, *Dangers of Sugar*, published in 1998, warns...

> or

> "In the article 'Top Swimmers in America,' Jane Smith reported in the current edition of *Sports Illustrated* that..."

Build the ethos of the source/author. If the author or researcher is not familiar to your audience, you may wish to spend a few moments building the ethos or credibility of the person. Do this *before* you document the evidence. Here's a brief example:

"Jane Smith has been a sportswriter for 22 years. She has specialized in swimming sports and has interviewed all the biggest Olympic swimming stars in the past 18 years." (ethos building)...(pause)...

"In the article 'Top Swimmers in America,' Jane Smith reported in the current edition of *Sports Illustrated* that..." (documentation)

Give an adequate amount of statistics/expert testimony. You should present at least one statistic or expert testimony to prove each main point of your speech. Don't go overboard, however. You can reach a point of diminishing returns, and an avalanche of statistics and expert testimony can overwhelm an audience. You need to be the judge of how much evidence to present to a particular audience.

Provide quality evidence. Your evidence should reflect the best possible research available. Are the authors credible? Are the sources of the information—books, magazines, periodicals—credible? If the quality of your information is questionable, the impact of your speech is jeopardized.

Provide recent evidence. Present research that is recent. Whenever possible, give research that is no older than five years. The more recent the evidence is, the more credible it is to your audience.

Provide relevant evidence. Test your evidence to ensure that it does indeed support your proposition or main point. After you have presented a piece of evidence, your audience should not have to ask themselves the question, "So what? What did that evidence have to do with the point he was trying to make?" Make the relevance of your evidence clear.

Restate your evidence in your own words. After you have stated your evidence or your expert testimony, it is important that you pause for a moment and then restate the information in your own words. This gives the audience another chance to be exposed to the data in a different way. Watch how the speaker restates the evidence in the following example:

> "The study indicated that 16 percent of women showed signs of stress, whereas 33 percent of the men in the experiment displayed stress." (evidence)...(pause)... *"What that means is* that twice as many men as women exhibited stress in the test." (restatement)

Translate your evidence into a picture. Sometimes the evidence you present is difficult to envision or comprehend. In such instances, it is important to translate or interpret the evidence in terms that are more readily understood or visualized by your listeners. Notice how the translation of the statistic provides a clearer picture. "The NASA space capsule weighs 120,000 pounds. That's the equivalent of 48 Toyota pickups!"

Other Forms of Reasoning

There are three other forms of reasoning we should briefly mention because they are often used in persuasive appeals logic. They are reasoning by analogy, reasoning by causation, and reasoning by definition.

> *Reasoning by analogy* is a reasoning attempt that shows that similar circumstances produce similar conclusions. This is a special form of reasoning by generalization. Suppose that Company A went bankrupt last year, and you show that the circumstances of Company A were similar to those of Company B. From that, you could assert that Company B will also go bankrupt. Because its circumstances are similar, it will suffer a similar fate. Another example of reasoning by analogy is, "You're just like your brother, and you'll end up in jail just like he did too." Pretty grim, huh?
>
> *Reasoning by causation* assumes that every cause has an effect. When two things occur together frequently, we often assume that one caused the other. Let's say every time you go swimming you get a

headache. After a while, you might conclude that the swimming caused the headache. The *independent variable,* the swimming, causes the *dependent variable,* the headache. You need to be careful, however, about drawing such conclusions. Is there always a relationship between the two variables? Does the independent variable always precede the dependent variable? And could there be other variables (*confounding variables*) involved that you're not aware of, such as after swimming you always drink three warm glasses of brandy to ward off the cold? That could cause a headache for anyone. Be careful when you draw a conclusion when reasoning by causation.

And finally, *reasoning by definition* is another form of logic that needs to be mentioned. When a situation has all the characteristics that are usually associated with a term, we can then use the term to describe the product of those characteristics. That is reasoning by definition. For example, if Joe's Diner has delicious food, great service, and reasonable prices, we can say the restaurant is an excellent restaurant. Because good food, great service, and reasonable prices are all characteristics of an excellent restaurant, we can apply that term to Joe's Diner. Once again, be careful when using this form of logic. Sure, Joe's Diner satisfies those three criteria presented, but what about the sanitation of the kitchen, the location of the restaurant, and the overall atmosphere of the place? Be careful with this form of reasoning also.

Pathos (Emotional Appeal)

Do you always base your decisions on sound reasoning and well-researched evidence? Where you vacation? Which car to buy? Where to go to dinner? Whom to invite to your party? Where to live? Whom to marry? Should you have children? Should you stay married? These and thousands of other questions confront you during your lifetime.

How do you make these decisions? Do you decide on the basis of advice from others, as you consider their credibility or ethos? Perhaps you base your decisions on logical reasoning and thorough research by emphasizing logos or logical proof. Or do you base your decisions on your "gut feelings," relying primarily on how you feel emotionally about an issue? Most people probably use a combination of all three in decisions of magnitude or importance, but research has shown that much decision making is ultimately based on emotional responses, personal tastes, needs, and desires. This is what Aristotle referred to as pathos, or emotional proof.

The third and final persuasive proof is pathos, or emotional appeal. *Pathos* appeals to the listener's needs, desires, and wishes. Whereas logos, or logical appeal, aims for the listener's head, pathos directs its efforts toward the listener's heart. In addition to providing logical reasoning, supported by sound evidence, and presenting yourself as a credible speaker, you must appeal to the emotions of your audience in your persuasive speech.

Hierarchy of Needs

Because emotional appeals deal with an individual's psychological needs, we should begin with an examination of the various needs. An introduction to this area is Abraham Maslow's *hierarchy of needs,* a psychological model of need structure depicting the lowest-level physical needs to the highest-level actualization needs.

The lowest level of the hierarchy is our *physical needs,* such as our need for food, water, air, sleep, and physical comfort. Our most basic requirements to get adequate oxygen to breathe, food to eat, and water to drink are often taken for granted, unless we are drowning, starving, or dying of thirst. Our audience will most likely have these most basic needs met, so a persuasive speech based primarily on the satisfaction of this level of need is not usually advised.

The second level on the hierarchy is *safety needs.* Safety needs not only include physical safety, such as freedom from illness, disease, and violence, they also include having a job, a place to call home, a sense of stability and order, and a lawful environment. Many persuasive appeals can be generated from this level of safety needs.

Belonging needs serve as the third level of needs. These include the need to be loved by a significant other and the need for family and friends. They also include the need to belong to a group of people who share your interests and activities, such as a church, an interest group, a pottery class, and even a motorcycle club. They can also include the need to belong to a political movement, a nation, or even the human race.

The fourth level is *self-esteem needs.* The assumption here is that people need to feel good about themselves. They need to feel they are worthwhile, attractive, capable, and skilled. People will invest a great amount of energy, effort, and money in activities that will enhance their self-esteem. Self-help books, diet centers, graduate schools, promotions at work, meditation retreats, jewelry stores, German auto centers, exclusive designer-clothing boutiques, and a thousand other self-esteem-enhancing sources cry out to us. This level of needs is rich in emotional-appeal material.

Self-actualization involves realizing one's highest potential. It is placed at the top level of the hierarchy of needs. We have a need to be the best we can with what we have been given. To be the best parent possible. The best teacher. The best spouse. To write that book we've been thinking about for years. Or to learn to fly an airplane.

A woman returned to school after having been away from formal education for more than 25 years. Even though she was at the age most people retire from work, she wanted to begin her college education to become a chiropractor. After raising three children by herself and saving for her college education, she was ready to accomplish what she had dreamed of for years. This woman was striving for self-actualization—realizing her highest desire, to become a person who helps heal others.

Some of the best emotional-appeal stories you can include in your speech will come from the lives of individuals who have sought to realize their highest potential. When you are researching emotional appeals for your persuasive speech, remember the various needs of your audience members.

Specific Emotional Targets

You should consider five other areas when preparing your emotional appeals to a particular audience. They are sex, conformity, wealth, pleasure, and personal growth.

Appealing to the motive of *sex* is one of the most popular strategies utilized by the advertising industry. Every other advertisement has an attractive man or woman fondling products from cars to fertilizer. Our desire to be attractive to others makes for a powerful motivational appeal. Beneath the motive of sex is a deeper need for intimacy, belonging, and love. These needs all provide rich areas to explore for emotional appeals.

Conformity is one of the most powerful needs we have. The need to appear and behave like others is a potent motivational force, affecting young and old alike. Often the appeal can take the form of avoiding nonconforming behavior or being different from everyone else. "You wouldn't want to be the only person in your neighborhood who didn't have attractive landscaping!" and "How would it feel to be the only person who didn't contribute, when all of your colleagues had?" are examples of this technique.

Another specific target that is especially effective with audiences is *wealth*. Wealth not only includes the desire to possess piles of money, diamonds, and gold; it also encompasses an individual's need to earn, save, and invest money. It can speak to a desire to spend money wisely and prevent its loss. Appeals to wealth can prove beneficial in moving your audiences emotionally.

Another motive you should consider is that of *pleasure*. Most people like doing things that bring them happiness, enjoyment, and pleasure. Use appeals that point out or highlight how your proposition will provide them with pleasure.

Personal growth is the individual's need or desire to examine life, explore different aspects of selfhood, and, hopefully, make strides toward growing as a human being. The emphasis is on becoming different from what we were in the past and exploring new ways of living and being. The introvert becomes the extrovert, the thinker becomes the feeler, and the bodybuilder becomes the spiritual seeker. The focus is on process and growth. This need to expand, change, and grow is one of the most potent of all personal needs to appeal to in your audience. It was the reason this book was written.

Suggestions for Using Emotional Appeals

When using emotional appeals, consider the following suggestions:

Select appropriate emotional appeals. You must analyze your topic and audience carefully, then research appropriate emotionally appealing material that will support your proposition and appeal to the needs of the audience.

Establish common ground with the audience. An audience will more likely listen to your emotional appeals if they feel you have things in common with them. During the first half of your talk, usually in the introduction, relate to common experiences, values, beliefs, and circumstances that will establish common ground with your listeners.

Use the yes-response. The audience must ultimately agree with your point of view if you are to be successful in your persuasive speech. One effective technique that can lay the groundwork in the beginning for such an agreeable climate is the *yes-response*—a series of rhetorical questions constructed so that the audience is likely to answer "yes." As the audience silently considers each question, they begin to get into a more agreeable state of mind. Listen to the series of questions this speaker uses for a speech on increasing the size of the police force in a certain town as he utilizes the *yes-response.*

"Do you want a town that is free from crime?

Would you like to be able to walk the streets at night again?

And wouldn't you want to feel safe in your own neighborhood?"

Use emotional appeal at the end of the body. If you are going to fully develop an emotional appeal, such as a story or long illustration, do so toward the end of your speech. The final main point in the body of your speech is the most appropriate place to include a detailed story. The first two main points should stress evidence and expert opinion as you present your arguments, but save the final point for material that is especially appealing to the emotions of the audience.

Match your nonverbal behavior with your appeal. Your body movement, gestures, voice, and facial expressions should reinforce the emotional appeals you are using. If your material is sad, look, talk, and move as if you are sad. If the material is joyous, look, talk, and move as if you are joyous. Don't give your audience mixed messages. Use your nonverbal communication to add credibility and impact to your verbal message.

Use pauses in your delivery. One common mistake speakers commit when delivering emotional appeals is forgetting to give the audience time to digest the material. Use pauses after you've delivered a powerful line of dialogue. A two- or three-second pause will give your audience time to consider what you have just said. It places emphasis on your statement, and it gives you time to breathe. Use your pauses as you practice the speech. If you don't practice the speech with pauses, you will forget to use them when the real speech time arrives.

TYPES OF PERSUASIVE SPEECHES

Now that we have looked at the basics of persuasive speaking—ethical proof, logical proof, and emotional proof—we can examine the basic main-point outlines of various persuasive speeches. The introductions, conclusions, and subpoints of the following outlines have been omitted.

Speech of Reasons Approach

If your audience has no opinion, is neutral, or is only mildly in favor or mildly opposed to your proposition, you can use the *speech of reasons* approach. This simple method of persuasive speaking is best suited for these audiences.

> *Proposition:* You should exercise regularly.
> I. Regular exercise will improve your physical health.
> II. Regular exercise will improve your psychological well-being.
> III. Regular exercise will improve your chances of living a long life.

Problem-Solution Approach

If you want your audience to consider the adoption of a specific plan or solution to a problem, you can use the *problem-solution* approach. This works best with an audience that has no opinion, is neutral, or is only mildly in favor or mildly opposed to your proposition.

> *Proposition:* You should support the eight percent federal income tax plan.
> I. The current federal income tax is unfair.

II. The proposed 8 percent federal income ta
equally.

III. The proposed 8 percent federal income ta
to our tax problem.

Monroe's Motivated Sequence

A more developed persuasive speech pattern is called *Monroe's Motivated Sequence,* developed by speech professor Alan Monroe in the 1930s. This pattern is especially useful if you are seeking immediate action or results from your audience. Monroe's Motivated Sequence has five steps—attention, need, satisfaction, visualization, and action. In the first step, you gain the audience's *attention* (introduction). In the second step, you make the audience feel a *need* for change by showing there is a serious problem to solve (body). In the *satisfaction* step, you present a solution to the problem (body). In the fourth step, you have the audience *visualize* the benefits of the solution you presented (body). And finally, state what *action* must be taken to implement the solution.

Proposition: You should support MADD with a $10 donation this month.
I. *Attention:* A local child is killed by a drunken driver.
II. *Need:* You or someone you love could be killed or injured by a drunken driver.
III. *Satisfaction:* Mothers Against Drunk Drivers (MADD) is a national organization that brings attention to this serious problem and supports legislation to get drunk drivers off the road.
IV. *Visualization:* Imagine our highways without drunk drivers where you and your loved ones are safe.
V. *Action:* I want you to support MADD with a $10 donation this month.

Criteria-Satisfaction Approach

If your audience is hostile to your proposition, this method can be effective because it utilizes the yes-response as you have them agree with your criteria for a satisfactory solution. It also seeks to establish common ground with your hostile audience, because you stipulate criteria that are agreeable to speaker and audience.

Proposition: You should attend a community college.
I. You want a college that meets these criteria.
A. It must offer a wide variety of courses.
B. It must offer individualized instructional support.
C. It must be affordable.

II. The community college meets these criteria.
   A. It offers a wide variety of courses.
   B. It offers individualized instructional support.
   C. It is affordable.

Negative Method

If your audience is hostile, the *negative method* can be especially effective, because the structure forces the audience to realize that there is no other option than the one you propose. Your main-point structure eliminates the other options as viable solutions.

Proposition: You should save money for the future.
   I. Your current level of savings is inadequate.
   II. The Social Security system will be bankrupt.
   III. Your earning power will diminish in coming years.
   IV. The only solution is to save money now for the future.

Sample Persuasive Speech Outline
You Should Invest in Mutual Funds

Proposition: You should invest in mutual funds.

Introduction

Would you consider investing just 80 cents a day now in order to earn $300,000 in the future? Have you wanted to get ahead financially, but were discouraged because you didn't think you had the money to invest? Or did you ever wish to play the stock market, but were afraid you didn't possess the knowledge or time to study the thousands of stocks you would have to choose from? Well, today I want to convince you to invest in mutual funds, because of their safety, profitability, and the ease of investment.

Body

I. *The first reason you should invest in mutual funds is their safety.*
   A. Charles Smith, in his book *The 100 Best Investments for Your Retirement*, states that "Mutual funds offer the safest stock investment vehicle available today."
   B. Unlike single stock investment, mutual funds are diversified among many different stocks.
   C. David D'Arcangelo, in his book *Wealth Starts at Home*, says, "Mutual stock funds have proven to give the small investor his safest way to play the market."
   D. Story about my uncle who lost his savings by investing in only one stock.

II. *The second reason you should invest in mutual funds is their profitability.*
   A. Tod Barnhart, in his book *A Kick in the Assets,* reports that "Historically stocks return nearly 11% annually (8% stock rise and 3% dividends). This outperforms the traditional savings passbook and IRA accounts 3 to 1."
   B. Show graph of 20-year returns for savings accounts versus mutual funds.
   C. Share story about my personal investment returns with mutual funds.
III. *The third reason you should invest in mutual funds is their ease.*
   A. You don't have to possess knowledge of the stock market, because mutual funds are handled by professional investment managers.
   B. In his book, *How to Retire Rich,* James O'Shaughnessy feels that "Mutual funds are the easiest way to invest your money in the stock market, especially when you invest a little each month."
   C. You can have your contribution deducted automatically from your paycheck.
   D. Share hypothetical story of individual investing $50 a month until retirement.

Conclusion

Today, I've shared with you three reasons why you should consider investing in mutual funds. First, they are safe. Second, they are profitable. And finally, they are easy to invest in. With as little as a $25 or $50 investment each month, your mutual fund can give you $300,000 by the time you retire. Isn't it worth it to set aside a few cents a day so you won't have to worry about your financial future in the years to come? Don't let this opportunity pass you by. Look into mutual funds as a way of insuring your future.

Bibliography

Tod Barnhart. *A Kick in the Assets.* New York: G. P. Putnam's Sons, 1998.
David D'Arcangelo. *Wealth Starts at Home.* New York: Dell, 1997.
James O'Shaughnessy. *How to Retire Rich.* New York: Broadway Books, 1998.
Charles Smith. *The 100 Best Investments for Your Retirement.* Holbrook, MA: Adams Media Publishing Group, 1998.

COMMUNICATION ACTIVITIES

Personal Activities

1. **The most persuasive speaker**

   Who is the most persuasive speaker you have ever heard? What made this person so persuasive? How did his ethos, logos, and pathos influence or shape your response to him or her? What personality characteristics and delivery skills do you share with this individual? What delivery skills and personality characteristics are different?

2. **A topic or belief you would die for**

   One of the most difficult assignments for the novice speaker is to select a persuasive topic. A method that is helpful in choosing such a topic is to ask yourself the questions—"What (if anything) would I die for? What would I risk my life for?" These two questions could provide some possible topics for your talk. If you discover that you wouldn't die for anything, or at least risk your life for something, maybe you should stick to informative speaking. Persuasive speaking, really good persuasive speaking, usually involves a speaker who is committed to something, stands for something, and is willing to sacrifice for something.

3. **Analyzing a persuasive appeal**

   Select three full-page ads in one of your favorite magazines, and examine each ad for the kinds of persuasive appeals it is attempting to evoke in the reader. Use Aristotle's three proofs (ethos, logos, and pathos) or Maslow's hierarchy of needs to identify and discuss the persuasive appeals found in each of the three ads you selected.

Class Activities

1. **Group discussion: Advertising campaign**

   Divide the class into groups of five or six. Each group is to design a simple, one-page advertisement attempting to get high school seniors to enroll in a public speaking course during their first semester in college. Use any of the information in this chapter to give you ideas as you design this one-page ad. Be prepared to present your ad to the entire class. Your instructor may have each group write and/or draw its ad on an overhead transparency so it can be viewed by all the students.

2. **"I want you to" speech**

   Prepare, practice, and present a six-to-eight-minute persuasive speech on the topic "I want you to..." In this speech, you could persuade your audience to visit a place, contribute to a charity, enroll in a particular class, or read a certain book. It's up to you! Research the topic, and interview experts in the field you are discussing. Develop each of your main points with documented information, examples, and strong emotional appeals. Include any visual aids that might be helpful. Your speech should contain an introduction, body, and conclusion.

3. **Problem-solution speech**

   Prepare, practice, and present a six-to-eight-minute persuasive speech discussing a problem of at least countywide importance and presenting a specific solution to that problem. Research the topic, and interview experts in the field you are discussing. Make certain that you prove there is a problem and that your solution will solve the problem. Develop each of your main points with documented information, examples, and strong emotional appeals. Include any visual aids that might be helpful. Your speech should contain an introduction, body, and conclusion.

4. **Monroe's Motivated Sequence speech**

   Prepare, practice, and present a six-to-eight-minute persuasive speech using Monroe's Motivated Sequence (attention, need, satisfaction, visualization, and action). Research the topic, and interview experts in the field you are discussing. Develop your main points with documented information, examples, and strong emotional appeals. Include any visual aids that might be helpful. Your speech should contain an introduction, body, and conclusion.

10

BECOMING A SPEAKER
A Lifelong Journey

Mario glanced around the room as the members of the family reunion committee sat silently staring at the floor. His Uncle Frank had just asked for a volunteer to serve as the master of ceremonies for the upcoming family reunion. It was going to be a weekend affair, with more than 80 family members in attendance. The hotel meeting room had been reserved, the caterer selected, and the entertainment committee formed. The only thing left to do was have someone volunteer to serve as master of ceremonies for the festivities on Saturday night.

Uncle Frank asked a second time for a volunteer, and again everyone remained silent, motionless. During that moment, Mario recalled the words of his public speaking teacher, who said, "Speaking is a lifelong skill. When the opportunities arise, choose to speak. Don't remain silent."

Mario's decision to speak did not come easily. He didn't feel like taking on the responsibilities of hosting Saturday night's events. He didn't feel like getting those butterflies again, as he did in his public speaking class. But Mario raised his hand, despite his feelings of anxiety and uncertainty.

Everyone in the room smiled and breathed a sigh of relief when Mario volunteered—everyone except for Mario. His journey was just beginning.

TWO WAYS OF VIEWING PUBLIC SPEAKING

Public Speaking—Never Again

Many public speaking students regard their final speech as exactly that— THEIR FINAL SPEECH. Never again will they have to research a speech.

Never again will they have to practice a speech. Never again will they have to stand before an audience. Never again will they have to experience those butterflies. Never again will they have to give another speech as long as they live. NEVER AGAIN, they reassure themselves.

From this perspective, public speaking can be viewed with anxiety, fear, and even anger, especially if it's a required course. It's seen as a necessary evil, something to be endured. It's a once-in-a-lifetime event. Like the measles—something to be survived, and then quickly pushed from our minds and forgotten. NEVER AGAIN.

Becoming a Speaker—A Lifelong Journey

There's another way to view your public speaking experience that is very different from the one just described. Instead of seeing it as an experience to be endured or tolerated, it can be seen as an invitation to a journey that may last your entire lifetime. Rather than a destination to be reached and then forgotten, it can be viewed as the beginning of a process of discovery and enrichment.

Becoming a speaker can be a lifelong journey to discover greater self-expression, gain increased personal power, and achieve a more intimate sense of who you are and where you're going. It can be the beginning of a wonderfully exciting journey that can take you to places you have never seen, put you in touch with people you have yet to meet, and introduce you to parts of yourself you never knew existed. Your decision to continue becoming a speaker—to stand in front of an audience and share a few words in the months and years to come—may make all the difference in your life.

When Mario listened to Uncle Frank's plea for a master of ceremonies in the opening story, he could have chosen to keep his eyes riveted to the ground like the rest of the family and let the opportunity pass.

Instead, he chose to raise his hand and volunteer. He chose to continue his journey to speak in front of others, instead of filing away his newly acquired skills with all the other classes he had taken in college. Although other students in his class may have been far more skillful and animated in their presentations, that didn't prevent Mario from continuing his journey.

Rather than close the door on the oral-presentation skills he had learned in the course and limit his speaking to the five speeches he had given in class, Mario chose to include just one more speech—about the family reunion. He decided to take another step in becoming a speaker for a lifetime.

When Saturday night rolled around, Mario gave a three-minute impromptu speech on the importance of family in this day and age. He introduced each entertainment skit with a funny quotation and concluded the evening's festivities with a brief speech on the importance of staying connected to one another.

By the end of the night, Mario was relieved it was over. He had been anxious before the evening began, but once he started speaking, he discovered he was actually enjoying the experience—the laughter, the tears, and the applause from the audience. And the congratulations on a job well done from Uncle Frank.

In the years that followed, Mario volunteered to present extra-credit oral reports in his other college classes. He volunteered to join the speakers' bureau when he worked for the phone company during his first years out of college. And Mario served as master of ceremonies numerous times for anniversaries, wedding receptions, and one retirement dinner, Uncle Frank's.

Mario continues on his lifelong journey as a speaker, for he is currently the teacher of 31 fourth-grade students at a little elementary school somewhere in the rolling hills of the California coast. Each day he stands in front of those fourth graders and teaches, encourages, entertains, and heals them with his words.

Because Mario chose to continue becoming a speaker, his life is much different from what it might have been. Your public speaking experience and your role as a speaker don't have to end with this course. You can chose to continue the journey. Perhaps for a lifetime.

BENEFITS OF BECOMING A LIFELONG SPEAKER

Maybe you're shaking your head and saying that's not for you. Who'd want to stand and speak in front of a room full of fourth graders? Or, for that matter, who'd want to pursue any profession requiring you to speak in front of an audience?

Perhaps being a teacher, lawyer, politician, or pastor are not among the careers you're considering at this moment, but hold on. Becoming a speaker—using your speaking skills after this course is over—doesn't necessarily mean you have to deliver a formal speech from a podium. Consider some of the many benefits you may derive from using the skills you've learned in this course.

Educational Benefits

You can put your speaking skills to use by volunteering to give extra-credit presentations, facilitating student learning groups, participating in class discussions, and leading student study groups. Your organizational and delivery skills will also enhance your chances for admission to graduate and professional schools when oral interviews are required of prospective candidates.

Career Benefits

Your speaking skills will impress interviewers when you are applying for future employment. And once you are on the job, your speaking skills (and your willingness to speak) will distinguish you from the majority of employees, who are inexperienced in and fearful of public speaking. Whether it's making a formal sales presentation or simply stating a point during a business meeting, the skills you have learned in this class will enable you to communicate your thoughts and ideas effectively and convincingly. Individuals who are skilled and willing to communicate are the ones who will be successful in the workplace.

Community Benefits

Not only will your educational and professional careers be enhanced by your speaking skills, your involvement in your community can also be increased. Rather than sitting silently at community meetings listening to other people talk, you can use your speaking skills to express your views and opinions at city council meetings, neighborhood gatherings, school board meetings, and church functions.

Personal-Contribution Benefits

Given the reluctance of most people to speak in front of an audience, your personal contribution to special occasions during your lifetime can be enormous. While the majority of people would rather die than face an audience, you can volunteer to speak at anniversary parties, wedding receptions, birthday celebrations, housewarmings, ground-breaking ceremonies, retirement dinners, engagement parties, political fund-raisers, company retreats, and award ceremonies. You can also volunteer to speak at baptisms, weddings, and funerals, all manner of rituals and celebrations from birth to death.

The speaking skills you have learned do not have to be filed away with the completion of your final speech in class, but can be used for the rest of your life. Public speaking is not a destination. It can be a lifelong process, if you choose.

Personal-Growth Benefits

If you choose to use your public speaking skills after this course, there's no guarantee you'll get rid of the butterflies completely. But the butterflies will fly in formation. With future practice and experience in public speaking, your ability and willingness to speak in front of others will increase. And your fear of the audience will decrease. Not completely. But with each speech, your fear will fade a little, and be replaced with an increased interest in your audience and how your message is being received. With each speech you will move from a self-centered frame of reference to an other-centered perspective.

Right now, with five or six speeches under your belt, you're probably still focused on how YOU did on your speech. How many mistakes YOU made in your presentation. How YOU came across to the audience. The focus is still probably on YOU. But as you gain speaking experience in the years to come, this preoccupation with self will gradually give way to an increased awareness and focus on THEM—your audience. You will move from YOU to THEM.

And isn't this one of life's most important lessons—to be less focused on self and more concerned with others? Our development from infancy, with its emphasis on total self-satisfaction, to maturity, with its sensitivity to the needs and desires of others, is one of the most significant developmental transitions we navigate in our lifetime.

In this respect, continuing your speaking can be extremely significant to your personal development. It can provide you with an ongoing opportunity to confront your fears of evaluation and rejection, and realize they are just that—fears—and not the actual responses from your audience. You'll begin to discover that in most cases, the audience will wish you well and welcome the messages you bring to them, whether it's a formal sales presentation or a story shared around a campfire.

In the years to come, you will be given many opportunities to speak in front of others. It may be just a few words of thanks at a business luncheon or a formal presentation at a professional conference. It may be sharing a story at a family reunion or delivering a commencement address at a graduation ceremony. Whatever the situation, these speaking opportunities will present themselves to you. What will you do? Will you remain silent? Or will you stand and speak? These are very simple acts—remaining silent, or standing and speaking. But acts that, by their very nature, will determine the individual you will become.

DEVELOPING THE HEART OF A SPEAKER

We began this book by discussing the significance of communication in your life and how your attitude is more important than your aptitude—your heart is more important than your head. And that's how we're going to end this book—by talking about your heart and the role it plays in your becoming a speaker for a lifetime.

You can acquire the knowledge and technical skills necessary to organize and deliver a speech, but if your attitude or heart is wrong, the speech will lack a certain vitality, wholeness, and impact. If your heart is one of insincerity, indifference, animosity, or arrogance, the audience will intuitively sense this and regard you with caution, defensiveness, and, in some cases, even hostility.

But if your heart is sincere, positive, and helpful, the audience will receive you in a more open, receptive, and friendly manner. Your audience is much more aware of and sensitive to your attitude than you might suspect.

Carl Jung, the famous psychiatrist, believed that it was the integrated personality or soul of the therapist that ultimately brought healing to the injured or disintegrated soul of the patient. He felt that beneath the words in therapy, it was the healthy heart of the therapist that somehow reached out, touched, and brought wholeness to the unhealthy heart of the patient. All the talking, analyzing, theorizing, and interpreting in therapy were secondary to the mysterious, powerful, and silent music of the heart. Perhaps this offers some insight into why certain individuals are draining to be around, while others are a joy to be near. Could it be that our hearts communicate to one another in ways we are not yet aware?

It's not enough to know how to research and organize a speech and deliver it without passing out from fright; you must possess an attitude or heart that communicates a positive message to the minds and hearts of your listeners. How does a speaker do this? Are some people born with the right attitude and others not? What are the ingredients that make for this kind of heart?

As you may have guessed, there are no easy answers to these questions. Maybe this topic doesn't readily lend itself to simple definition or logical explanation. Perhaps what we can't define, measure, and dissect should be left alone. But we all know that unmistakable feeling when our hearts have been touched by the words or actions of another. Maybe you experienced this sensation during one of the speeches you listened to this semester in your public speaking course. That moment when the communication between speaker and listener transcended even language itself.

Although there is no clear-cut map into this territory of the heart, there are three ingredients or dispositions of the speaker that seem to bring the speaker closer to the hearts of the listeners. The speaker needs to love the topic he is speaking about. The speaker needs to love the audience. And the speaker needs to love him- or herself. Ideally, a speaker could possess each of these three ingredients, but at least one of these three is necessary to touch the hearts of the listeners.

The Speaker Needs to Love the Topic

A romantic affection for the topic is not what we're talking about here. It's more of a passion for or commitment to the subject. The topic of any speech you give in the future must be important to you—something you feel strongly about, committed to. Anything less will not motivate you to speak well nor compel your audience to listen deeply. If you don't feel strongly about something, don't waste the audience's time. You and your audience have other things to do, and life is short.

It's easy to say the speaker needs to love the topic, but maybe it's easier said than done. If you were given a blank piece of paper, a pencil, and three minutes, how many topics could you list that would fit this requirement? A recent study of college freshmen and sophomores found the average respondent could list only five topics that fit this description. Of all the thousands of things to list, most students could list only five. How many could you list?

As children, we loved just about everything we came in contact with—a butterfly, a creek, the smell of rain on asphalt, color crayons, and puppies. But as we grew older, this list grew smaller with each ensuing year. So why is it years later we can list only five topics we love? What happened to our love affair with life?

In the future, you will be given many opportunities to speak in front of others. Don't speak unless you really care about the topic. But you also might want to examine the things and people you really love. Have your interests and passions of the heart diminished over the years? Is there anything you get excited about anymore? Don't let your heart become hard as you get older. Discover ways to remain open to life, to get excited and thrilled about the countless events and miracles that happen to you daily.

Whether it's giving a toast at a wedding reception or delivering a formal presentation to a scientific conference, your heart should reflect a love or passion for the topic at hand. If it doesn't, don't speak. If your heart's not really involved, then don't speak. Wait until the opportunity to toast a couple you care about or wait until you discover a scientific topic that you feel deeply about before you walk up to the podium. Your love for the topic, regardless of what it is, will be communicated to your audience, beyond your words.

Much of what passes for public speaking in this culture is really mediocre, unimpressive, and boring. Many of our professors, preachers, and politicians have lost their passion, and their lectures, sermons, and speeches reflect their weary hearts. Don't add to this debris. Remember to speak about topics you feel a passion for, or remain silent.

The Speaker Needs to Love the Audience

The audience is not the enemy. If that's all you learn from this book, you will have gotten your money's worth. And more. You see, the audience is like a Rorschach test. You know, the famous inkblot test. A person looks at an inkblot on a piece of paper and is asked to describe what she "sees." Some people see a monster. Others describe a train. And still others see a beautiful butterfly.

Of course, there is no correct answer, because there is no "picture." Just a blot of ink squished between two halves of a cardboard screen. What the individual "sees" is really "who" that individual is. The paranoid man "sees" a dark, ominous monster. The divorced woman "sees" a train leaving a station. And the young bride "sees" a beautiful butterfly. It's been said that "We don't see the world the way the world is. We see the world the way we are." How true this is.

And "how" we are when we are novice speakers is inexperienced. The audience is more than just a collection of people who have assembled to listen to our speech. They can be seen as the ENEMY. Not the kind of enemy who will hurt us physically, but the enemy who will laugh at our mistakes, judge our inadequacies, and reject our opinions. The audience represents many of our deepest fears—fears of evaluation, rejection, and, ultimately, abandonment. The audience is the Rorschach test upon which we project all the fears we don't have names for, only that terrifying, empty feeling in the pit of our stomach.

But as you gain experience in speaking, you slowly realize the audience is not the enemy. The laughter occurs only when you say something funny. The judgment is usually expressed in their applause. And the rejection doesn't occur. Instead, our speeches are usually met with compliments and congratulations. If you were fortunate during this semester in public speaking, the responses from your audience were positive and supportive. And your perception of audience-as-enemy shifted to audience-as-friend or, at least, audience-as-nonthreatening acquaintance.

If you choose to become a speaker for your lifetime—to give speeches after the end of your public speaking course—your impact on your audience will be greatly enhanced if you can learn to love your audience.

The Speaker Needs to Love Himself/Herself

You will touch the hearts of the audience if they sense you love yourself. Not with a self-absorbed, narcissistic kind of love. Nor an arrogant, boastful kind of love either. But, rather, an attitude of gentleness or softness toward yourself. An attitude of spaciousness. An attitude that says you don't have to be perfect when you speak. An attitude that says you can make mistakes as a speaker. You can be human. It's an attitude that says you don't have to be the best speaker, an impressive speaker, or even a good speaker. But more important, you can be a speaker with a message to share with an audience you are concerned about.

Loving yourself requires a softening toward yourself. An attitude of gentleness that isn't concerned so much with performance, action, or results as it is with supporting and nurturing your willingness to speak.

This love is also a softening to the fear or anxiety you may be feeling about speaking. Rather than tensing, hardening, and defending yourself against those butterflies in the stomach, it involves a process of welcoming, relaxing, and letting go. Softening allows your butterflies to fly wherever they want. Like watching children in a playground, you simply welcome the scene and do not attempt to control it. The paradoxical thing about accepting your fears is that they will have less control over you when you simply let them be. Don't try to get rid of them, redirect them, or control them. Give yourself permission to let them in for a while and notice what follows.

Finally, this love involves some level of acceptance of who you are. Your strengths and your weaknesses. Those things you do well and those things you don't do well. This acceptance of self requires a recognition of the fact that not everything you do has to be done well, or even done at all. And it requires a deeper appreciation for those so-called weaknesses. For it just might be that our weaknesses, whatever they may be, are the very aspects of ourselves that make us understanding, humble, caring, and connected to others. In the end, human.

When you speak in front of an audience, let them sense your love for the topic, your love for the audience, and your love for yourself. This may be your most important message in your journey to become a speaker for a lifetime.

FINAL COMMUNICATION ACTIVITY: IMPROMPTU SPEAKING

During your lifetime, the vast majority of your public speaking will be impromptu—speaking without prior preparation and practice. Very rarely will you be given an opportunity to research, outline, practice, and deliver a formal speech. Most of your speaking will be informal, less than three minutes, and delivered without preparation. Whether you're presenting your opinion at a city council meeting, responding to a question at a business meeting, or giving a toast at a family gathering, your speaking will most likely be on the spur of the moment. Every day you will be asked to present your thoughts and feelings during informal speaking situations. So our final communication activity will provide you with the five basic steps necessary for giving an impromptu speech.

The Five Steps of Impromptu Speaking

The secret of effective impromptu speaking is to have only one main idea to share with the audience and to present that idea in an organized fashion.

Step 1: Select One Thought
Your first step in impromptu speaking is to select *one* thought, idea, or theme. We'll divide that thought into smaller parts later. But first, select just one thought you wish to communicate to your audience. It can be as simple as "Greg has been kind to us" or "Speech training is helpful." Many experienced impromptu speakers use a quotation or proverb as their main idea or thought, such as "Love your neighbor" or "A stitch in time saves nine." No matter what topic you're given, try to think of a one-sentence (a short one at that) idea or thought to work with. The shorter the better.

Step 2: Organize Your Thought into a Pattern
Once you've decided on a main thought or idea, the second step in the impromptu process is to organize it into a pattern. Here is a list of some ways you can organize your topic:

Time order—past/present/future, then/now

Topical order—three characteristics about..., two reasons why we should...

Spatial order—near/far, up/down, kitchen/bedroom

Problem/solution—crime/education, inflation/reduce deficit

Let's try to organize the topic of "money" into the five organizational patterns listed above.

Time order	I. Money I had in the past.
	II. Money I currently have.
	III. Money I will have in the future.
Topical order	I. Money is difficult to earn.
	II. Money is easy to spend.
Spatial order	I. Inflation rates in America.
	II. Inflation rates in Brazil.
Problem/solution	I. Saving money is difficult.
	II. Enroll in a payroll-deduction program.

Notice how a single topic, such as "money," can be organized in a variety of patterns. With some practice, you can organize any topic into a number of patterns without much difficulty.

Step 3: Support Your Points with Specifics
Once you've selected your topic and have organized it into some pattern, you are ready to move to the third step of supporting the main

points of your impromptu speech. You can develop your main points with definitions, comparisons, specific examples, anecdotes, personal illustrations, statistics, facts, or quotations. One of the easiest methods of support is to reach back into your own life experience and share brief anecdotes or illustrations that relate to the point you are trying to make. This method helps the audience to feel more involved with you, the speaker.

Step 4: Construct an Introduction

Now that you've selected an impromptu topic, organized the topic into a main-point pattern, and developed each point with supporting material, you're ready to construct a brief introduction for your talk. The introduction will consist of an attention getter and a preview of main points. Your entire introduction should take no more than 10–15 seconds for a 90-second impromptu speech.

The attention getter can be an audience question, a personal statement of belief, or a brief anecdote. Review Chapter 6 for more information on attention getters. A preview of main points should follow your attention getter. This is simply a one-sentence statement of the two or three main points you want to present in your talk. For instance, "I'd like to tell you about two of Jane's wonderful traits—her dedication to her job and her dedication to her family."

Step 5: Construct a Conclusion

Your conclusion should contain a review of main points and a final thought or quotation. For a 90-second impromptu speech, the conclusion should be about 10–15 seconds long. The review of main points should be a one-sentence review of the two points you presented in your talk. For example, "This evening I've told you about Jane's dedication to her job and her dedication to her family." After you've reviewed your points, you end your speech with a final thought or appeal. Once again, you can review final-thought devices in Chapter 6.

One thing to remember about your conclusion is know when to end. Your conclusion should be short and to the point. Don't ramble. This is not the time to begin another point or share a second speech. Know when to put your impromptu speech to bed.

90-Second Impromptu-Speech Outline

Look at the outline of the impromptu speech presented below. Review each part of the outline to make sure you understand and visualize the function of each component. This basic outline can be used in all speeches, regardless of length.

Introduction (10–15 seconds)
> Attention getter
> Preview of main points

Body

> **I.** Main point (30 seconds)
>> Example, anecdote, or evidence
> **II.** Main point (30 seconds)
>> Example, anecdote, or evidence

Conclusion (10–15 seconds)
> Summary of main points
> Final thought

Some Final Words of Encouragement When Giving Impromptu Speeches

Keep Your Speech Short

If you are ever asked to give an impromptu speech, keep your speech short. If television advertisers are willing to spend hundreds of thousands of dollars for a 30- or 60-second advertising spot because they believe the message will reach their target audience, you should be able to get a thought or two across to your audience in one or two minutes.

Keep to Your Point

Untrained speakers seem to wander and ramble in their speeches. When you give an impromptu talk, stick to your points. This is not a time for digressions or tangents. The old saying "The less you say, the more you say. And the more you say, the less you say" applies here. Keep focused.

Keep It Organized

Follow the simple outline presented here. It will save you a great deal of decision making as you walk up to the podium. You won't have to think too much. Just fit your thoughts into the outline format, and you'll do just fine. Simplicity is the basis of all beauty.

Keep It Colorful

When you support your two main points with developmental material, remember to use colorful, descriptive language. Pretend that your audience is blind and your responsibility is to paint mental pictures in their minds as you speak. This technique will help you utilize colorful language.

Keep It Conversational

Use your regular conversational voice, but enlarge it a little so you will project to the people in the back of the audience. Don't try to sound like anyone else. Be yourself. Just enlarge it a bit. No one in the entire world has a voice pattern identical to yours, so enjoy your uniqueness.

Keep Your Cool

The natural tendency is to rush your impromptu speech, so remember to slow down. Walk to the podium slowly—there's no hurry. It will also give you time to organize your thoughts and locate supporting material from your life experience. Use pauses between the introduction, main points, and conclusion. Use pauses before and after important words or phrases. The use of pauses is one of the most powerful signs of speaker confidence.

Keep It Natural

Your delivery—your voice, body movement, gestures, and facial expression—should be natural and relaxed. You should talk to the audience as if you are talking with friends. Remember, the audience wants you to succeed. Relax and enjoy the experience. Be yourself.

Keep It in Perspective

This speech is only two minutes out of your entire life. If you live to age 72, you will have experienced 37,324,800 minutes. Okay, so 12,614,400 of them are probably spent sleeping, but that still leaves you with at least 24,710,400 minutes of waking time. In round numbers, that's 25 million minutes! Your impromptu speech in only two minutes in length. That's only 0.000000001 percent of your life. With all that time left, maybe you should give two impromptu speeches before you leave the planet. Anyway, in the light of eternity, it's not a big deal. Keep it in perspective.

Impromptu Word List

The following list of topics can be used for impromptu speaking practice. Select a number and decide on one of the two topics that follow it. Give yourself a few moments (or minutes) to prepare your speech using the five steps suggested. Then give your impromptu speech. You'll do well!

1. summer, friend	2. love, boy	3. ship, film
4. lamp, truth	5. telephone, sin	6. star, computer
7. watch, store	8. furniture, car	9. energy, book
10. people, newspaper	11. plant, vacation	12. marriage, ball
13. body, college	14. water, country	15. hate, furniture
16. animal, bed	17. ocean, art	18. freedom, girl
19. teacher, clothes	20. insect, jewelry	21. personality, bat
22. crime, carpet	23. police, season	24. mistake, home
25. monster, foreign	26. illness, shoe	27. spirit, family
28. happiness, salt	29. passion, boat	30. doctor, regret
31. money, food	32. secret, bill	33. weep, picture
34. weather, hair	35. single, door	36. gift, school
37. music, path	38. wish, floor	39. brother, map
40. history, mood	41. dog, society	42. father, hope
43. joy, sister	44. change, plane	45. tool, universe
46. talk, fun	47. holy, nation	48. plastic, wonder
49. crisis, travel	50. boundary, heart	51. shock, passage
52. nature, divorce	53. habit, philosophy	54. church, power
55. miracle, toy	56. gun, earth	57. moral, soap
58. temper, color	59. army, fear	60. ground, fish
61. logic, magazine	62. city, sensitive	63. farm, tax
64. parade, recess	65. paper, sex	66. worry, lamp

INDEX